The Ostrers &

Gaumont British

The Ostrers & Gaumont British

Nigel Ostrer

www.gaumontbritish.com

British Library Cataloguing in Publication Data
A catalogue record for this book is available
from the British Library.

Published by Nigel Ostrer
First published 2010
Copyright Nigel Ostrer 2009 (text)
All rights reserved

ISBN 978-0-9564822-1-1

Cover designed by Roman Klistinec

Printed and bound by Lulu Enterprises, Inc

ACKNOWLEDGEMENTS

Malcolm Baird
Jonathan Balcon
John Rank
Maria & Paul Talley
Andrew Fforde-Wilton
Timothy Fortuna
Katia Hadidian
Julie Harris
Domenico & Susan Iannaccone
Paul Kale
Roman Klistinec
Barbara Leese
Martina Oliver (Getty Images)
Darryl & Pam Ostrer
Edward & Susan Ostrer
Paul & James Ostrer
Andrew Spicer
Simon & Jane Taylor
Simon White

DEDICATION

To my sister, Iona Joseph, for her greatly appreciated help and encouragement.

CONTENTS

FOREWORD: by Malcolm Baird
(reproduced by kind permission of Malcolm Baird)

The name "Gaumont British" is well known to film historians but it means nothing to the average person under the age of 70. However, in the 1930s Gaumont British (GB) dominated the British film industry with its large chain of cinemas and its vast studio complex at Lime Grove. GB employed people of the calibre of Alfred Hitchcock, Rex Harrison and Margaret Lockwood. The person who "made it all possible" was a quiet-spoken and somewhat reclusive individual called Isidore Ostrer. Born in 1889 to a humble Jewish family in Whitechapel, he had made his first fortune in textiles during World War I, then he established a private bank, and in 1922 he took over the Gaumont film company from its French founders and renamed it Gaumont British. After a few years, talking pictures arrived and GB moved into its decade of glory, the1930s.

Nigel Ostrer is a nephew of the famous Isidore; his father Maurice was one of the five brothers most of whom had film connections, but Isidore was the dominant figure in the clan. This new book is a welcome change from the usual run of film history books which tend to be either memories of the stars (strong on film stills but weak on text) or statistical compilations featuring bar charts.

The first part of the book (Chapters 1-11) is on Isidore and the various Ostrer relatives. All too often family histories can be unreadable, but Nigel Ostrer's book is a refreshing exception. He evokes the various personalities in a colloquial style, laced with hilarious anecdotes and the occasional expletive.

The second part of the book (Chapters 12-24) sets out the history of Gaumont British. It owed its success not only to the astuteness of Ostrer but also to historical timing: the film industry was immensely boosted by the arrival of talkies in 1929, and cinema attendance also rose because of audiences' need for mental escape from the bad economic times and the growing troubles in Europe.

Early in 1932, GB quietly took over Baird Television Ltd. which had become financially precarious. As a result, Baird Television received a badly-needed infusion of capital which enabled it to hire some brilliant scientists with expertise in the new technology of electronic television, and to move to the Crystal Palace where a fully equipped television studio and ultra short wave transmitter were set up. After a boardroom coup in 1933 my father's position as managing director became nominal, although he was still well paid. Under the new arrangement he was relieved of administrative duties and this freed him to do full time research on large-screen and colour television. Ostrer felt that television could be part of his film empire, with live telecasts of sporting events being shown on cinema screens as an accompaniment to the main feature film. He and my father both felt that the BBC was acting as a dog-in-a-manger on television. They lacked the resources and the will to support it properly, but they were jealous of their legislated monopoly over broadcasting.

At the outbreak of World War II, all television was shut down. GB came under scrutiny by a Board of Trade enquiry and Ostrer also felt threatened by the possibility of German invasion. In 1940 he was named on the infamous Nazi death list, along with "people thought to be dangerous" such as Winston Churchill, J.B.Priestley and Noel Coward. In 1941 GB was sold to rival film magnate J.Arthur Rank;   all Gaumont cinemas were rebranded as Odeon cinemas. Ostrer moved to the USA for the war years and though he eventually returned to Britain he never made a major comeback in the film industry. His business interest returned to the textile industry in which he had started many years earlier. He lived on until 1975 in semi-seclusion.

On a technical note, this book is strongly commended for its readable type size and for the setting and captioning of the photographs. Under the guidance of Nigel Ostrer, the publishers have refrained from the modern tendency to miniaturise the photographs to almost postage-stamp size. The only negative comment concerns the lack of an index which could have helped the reader to navigate through the many names of the Ostrer clan and the others who were part of this fascinating story.

March 12, 2010

www.bairdtelevision.com

REVIEW by Dr Andrew Spicer
(reproduced by kind permission of Dr Andrew Spicer)

Dear Nigel,

I've just read with much interest your book *The Ostrers and Gaumont British*, which proves there is an audience and that scholars of British cinema will be grateful for your work. Thank you for writing this book and for helping to make the achievements of your family visible. As someone researching the role of film producers, I'm keenly aware that this story is an extremely important aspect of the British film industry and must not be neglected.

Best wishes,

Dr Andrew Spicer
Reader in Cultural History
School of Creative Arts
University of the West of England.

July 22, 2010

.

INTRODUCTION

Why did I write this book?

A year ago I purchased a DVD from the British Film Institute called "Silent Britain", which is a BBC-4 and BFI co-production. Though the DVD is informative, interesting and enjoyable, I was appalled by the omission of Leon Gaumont and the Gaumont British Picture Corporation. Leon produced hundreds of silent films in England from 1898, and he erected the first purpose-built film production studio in London in 1914, with a glass roof. By 1935 Gaumont British was the largest film production company in England, and in that year spent £1,200,000 on making films. Leon and Gaumont British were not mentioned at all in this DVD. But worse, to add insult to injury, the DVD showed a photograph of Leon's glass-roofed studio in West London and called it the Gainsborough Studio, which was in Islington in North London. The Gainsborough company was a subsidiary of Gaumont British.

To express my disgust, I wrote to the Chairman of the British Broadcasting Corporation and to the Director of the British Film Institute. I decided to start at the top and work my way down; fully expecting my letter to end up in the dustbin. In my letter I said it was unacceptably second-rate and unprofessional that the makers of this DVD did not bother to research the subject comprehensively. Adding that the result amounts to a re-write of history by omission.

There were 350 Gaumont cinemas in this country in the 1930s, but now there are none (not one) so-named, because J. Arthur Rank renamed most of the Gaumont cinemas as Odeon after he acquired control of both companies (Odeon and Gaumont).

The few cinemas that survived as Gaumonts have all gone, so there are no cinemas named Gaumont today. Needless to add, the Gaumont British studio complex erected in 1932 in Lime Grove, Shepherd's Bush, was used by BBC Television for over 40 years from 1949 to 1991. After which it was sold to a property developer who demolished the listed building and replaced it with a clump of small houses. So much for the relevance of listing buildings to preserve the country's historical or architectural heritage. By contrast, there is a museum dedicated to Gaumont in Paris, so the French take his contribution to film history more seriously.

Recently someone said to me, why are you bothering to write this book because no one is interested in reading about a company that closed down 60 years ago. It occurred to me that a considerable number of people are interested in the Titanic, which sank 95 years ago, and so there may be a few (perhaps only one or two) who are interested in the history of film production. Anyway, it seemed to me that there is an unwritten policy to air-brush Gaumont British out of history. So I decided to do something about it, after all I knew many of the people involved, and by recalling some of their idiosyncrasies and eccentric activities I hope to bring them to life and help to re-establish Gaumont British as a prominent pioneer in the history of film production.

I have never written a book before, but thought what the hell I'll have a go. Mind you, I don't read books because I prefer to spend my leisure time watching films on DVD and television.

This book is a personal (and unofficial) biography of my family who were pioneers in the development of the British film industry, and had a few fingers in early television and radio, as much as anyone could have in a government-controlled monopoly, which it was at that time. The bits about my family are based on my recollections and observations, with invaluable input from my sister, Iona. And the rest is history.

Readers of a sensitive disposition might find the occasional expletive offensive, but a lot of modern Hollywood films have the word "fuck" in every sentence, so much so that it is difficult to know what the actors are talking about, not that that is important, because such films are usually crap. I, however, toss in the occasional expletive to keep the readers awake, as a sort-of shock therapy, otherwise they might get a bit bored and nod off half way down a page. Also, it is very comforting to know I live in a country that respects freedom of speech, because sometimes when I express my opinion I use descriptive language which some readers may find a bit over the top.

Part One of this book is about the Ostrers. Part Two is about Gaumont British. Where possible I have included a black-and-white photograph of my relatives, some of the houses they lived in, and the studio complex and departments. Unfortunately not all of the photographs are high quality, but I decided it best to include everyone even though some of the family snaps are grainy, low resolution or small.

PART ONE

The Ostrers

My mother, Renee Clama, in The Man They Could Not
Arrest, directed by Michael Balcon. (1931)
(by kind permission of Hulton Archive/ Getty Images)

Chapter 1: THE OSTRER ROOTS

Let's begin at the beginning with my grandfather.

My paternal grandfather was born in 1862 as Jacob Ostrofsky. He was probably born in Poland, or maybe the Ukraine. No one seems to know which. My Uncle David (one of Jacob's sons) visited Poland in search of his roots, and I reckon he wouldn't have gone there unless he thought it was the right place to look. Also, I was told by someone who worked at Gaumont British and later went on to win an Oscar in Hollywood (as one does), the part of the Lime Grove studio complex in which the Ostrer brother's offices were located was known as The Polish Corridor.

An east-European friend told me that the border between Poland and the Ukraine has repeatedly changed from time-to-time as each country snatched a piece of the other's territory, or reclaimed territory previously abducted. Therefore a town in such a location would sometimes be in eastern Poland and at other times be in western Ukraine. My friend added that a name ending "fsky" sounds more Ukrainian than Polish. Also, he said "Jacob" sounds more Russian than Polish.

Anyway, Poland or the Ukraine or where ever he came from, Jacob moved to England before 1885. And thank God he did, otherwise we would have been gassed and incinerated in one of Hitler's ovens. Jacob lived at 16 Great Alie Street in Whitechapel, with his wife, Fanny (my grandmother), their children (my father, uncles and aunt), and Fanny's brother, Isidore Schaffer.

My grandfather worked as a boot riveter. Nowadays everyone seems to wear trainers, and so probably don't know what a boot is. Anyway, for strength and durability a part of the boot's construction was riveted together.   So my grandfather had a semi-skilled manual job working for a company that made boots.

Some time after 1885 he changed his name from Jacob Ostrofsky to Nathan Ostrer.   He probably changed his surname to Ostrer to make it sound less foreign (and easier to pronounce) than Ostrofsky. And at the same time he changed his first name from Jacob in memory of his son, Nathan, who died aged two in 1885.

After their arrival in England, my grandparents embarked on a rapid breeding program, producing six sons (one died) and one daughter.   My Aunt Sadie was the eldest, born in 1885, followed by Uncle David, the eldest of the Ostrer brothers, born in 1886.   Next was Uncle Isidore, who became leader of the clan, born in 1889.   Uncle Harry was born in 1890, followed by Uncle Mark, born in 1892.

**My paternal grandmother, Fanny Ostrer
and grandfather, Nathan Ostrer (insert).**
(by kind permission of the Ostrer Family Archive)

And last was my father, Maurice, born in 1896; the youngest in the family. His sister, Sadie, who was eleven years older than him, married and moved to New York. After leaving school, Maurice moved to New York too, where he was looked after by his sister. He told me he worked in an automat restaurant, restocking the food windows. In 1918, his brother Isidore had struck gold, and sent him the money to return to England first class.

At this point two different versions of the family history are available. Mine, and that of my cousin, Diana (she was Isidore's daughter, sort of). So, take your pick. According to Diana, my grandfather's son, Isidore (he was my uncle), married in 1914, and rented a house in Southend where he lived with his parents and brothers and sister. Whereas in fact the family moved in 1914 from Great Alie Street in Whitechapel to Acton House, Amhurst Road in Hackney.

Diana said they were so poor that they sometimes had to share one or two shirts amongst the five brothers. She also said, a bag of broken biscuits was a rare treat. However, one of the five, my father (Maurice), told me he had moved to New York in 1912, so he wasn't in Southend. And neither was his sister, Sadie (she was my aunt), who moved to New York earlier. If they were so impoverished how could they afford to pay Maurice's and Sadie's fares to New York; albeit steerage? If there were only enough clothes for one or two of the brothers to go to work, how could they pay the rent on this seaside house? And how could they pay the train fare to commute to work in London? Needless to add, the time scale of the Southend episode was before Diana was born.

I cannot imagine my Uncle Isidore (at the time a junior clerk) and his newly-wed wife, Helene, renting their own house and filling it up with his parents and brothers, walking about in his marital home half naked because they didn't have enough clothes.

Frankly, having to live with a swarm of in-laws from day one, semi-naked or otherwise, sounds to me like a recipe for instant divorce.

In my opinion, Diana's version does not add up. To me, it is a theatrical embellishment on the rags-to-riches theme that would go down well at the box office if Hollywood made a movie about my family history. I will consider offers in due course. Whereas my life has been downhill all the way from riches-to-rags, though I haven't reached the bottom, yet. Fortunately my decline in circumstances has been in relatively sumptuous comfort.

Chapter 2: ISIDORE STRUCK GOLD

Just in case you are getting confused, let me explain who is who again. Maurice Ostrer was my father, and my Uncle Isidore Ostrer was his older brother. Let's continue.

Uncle Isidore's sudden success was shrouded in mystery, and I never did find out exactly how he made it. Those in the family who knew, like my father, Maurice (he was Isidore's brother), were reluctant to reveal the full details. My father said Isidore was working as a junior clerk in a stockbroker's office. The wealthiest client was Rothschild, who dropped in one day, when all of the senior partners were out. Isidore, the junior clerk, was brought forward because he was the only person in the office who knew anything about the Rothschild account. Rothschild was so impressed with the service he received from Isidore, thereafter he insisted that he was always served by Isidore and not by the senior partners.

Apart from my father, no one else seemed to know how Isidore made it big time overnight. My mother (Renee) didn't know. She once told me that Isidore is God, and my father is the High Priest, protecting God. Isidore's secretary, who worked for him for fifty-two years, chose not to tell me because she felt it indiscreet to reveal such confidential information. And she was right, had she told me it would be in this book. Everyone called her Miss Holder, but her married name was Muriel Castells. In those days a secretary was always called "Miss" regardless of her marital status, and was always known by her maiden name. It was only years later that I learned her real surname, but anyway I always called her Muriel. She started work at the age of sixteen in the family's merchant bank, and continued to work for Isidore long after he had retired, as his housekeeper at Hills End in Sunningdale, until he died in 1975.

Hills End was a large isolated country house set in a few acres of garden that backed onto Sunningdale Golf Course. My father, Maurice, and his brother, my Uncle Isidore, shared this house for more than twenty years. I remember Muriel telling me how boring her life was living at Hills End during the winter months while Isidore and Maurice were in their rented flat in Cannes (South of France). She didn't drive and it was a long walk to the village, so she was cut off unless the chauffeur drove her about. The cook and the maids were always leaving (and difficult to replace) because there was nothing to do in an isolated country house in mothballs for six months of the year.

After Isidore died Muriel returned to her own home in

Hills End in Sunningdale, Berkshire.
(by kind permission of the Ostrer Family Archive)

Finchley and later moved to Bexhill-on-Sea. She was extremely nice and easy to get on with, and I visited her in Finchley and Bexhill on several occasions, and spoke with her on the telephone periodically and every Christmas, the last time was in 1999 two weeks before she died. I remember in this final conversation she mentioned that she was 97 years old, I was absolutely flabbergasted because she looked so much younger and I assumed she was in her 70s.

As it was so difficult to obtain details about how Isidore suddenly became wealthy, I presumed there was something to hide. I suspect it had to do with the supply of uniforms in the 1914-18 war, because Isidore struck gold during the war, and around that time bought control of a small woollen textile company, Illingworth Morris. He once told me that wool will always be in demand, especially in wartime, because soldiers uniforms and greatcoats are wool. Needless to add, he formulated this view before synthetic fibres came in.

At that time insider-trading was not illegal, there was no capital gains tax, and it was inexpensive to buy stock options, so I presume it was relatively easy for an astute person with reliable information to make a lot of money without any capital.

After the war Isidore started the Ostrer Brothers Bank, a private commercial bank. It was called Messrs. Ostrer Bros., and was located at 25-31 Moregate EC2. And in 1918 the family moved to Brighton, where my grandfather, Nathan (previously Jacob) died in 1932.

Chapter 3: HARRY, SADIE & DAVID

In this chapter I am covering the two minor Ostrer brothers, my Uncles Harry and David. They didn't move mountains. They didn't even climb mountains. They just shuffled along in the background behind Uncle Isidore Ostrer, as did their sister, Aunt Sadie.

In the early days, the Ostrer brothers travelled up to London every day on the same train from Brighton. Uncle Harry and my father, Maurice, fell out, and for two years stood some distance apart on the platform ignoring each other. The reason they fell out is because Harry was having an affair with a married woman who he later married after being named in the divorce. These sort of marital details were

My Uncle, Harry Ostrer, lived in Hove.
(by kind permission of the Ostrer Family Archive)

important at that time, whereas nowadays one can shack up with anyone and no one gives a fuck.

Uncle Harry, lived in Hove for the last 50 years of his life. He had been a school teacher and later worked with scripts at Gaumont British. Harry was literary editor of The Wicked Lady (1945), senario editor of Caravan (1946), and screenwriter of The Idol of Paris (1948). The latter was the only film produced by Premier Productions, and was a box-office flop.

They used scaffolding to support some of the film sets in the Lime Grove studio, and Harry came across a pile of scaffolding in the studio. Thinking it had been thrown out, he sold it to a scrap metal merchant. He thought he was being helpful, but the production team thought otherwise.

His step-daughter (my step-cousin), Glynis Lorrimer, was the Gainsborough lady, who sat in an oval picture frame nodding her head at the beginning of each film.

Aunt Sadie (my father's sister) worked her way through three marriages, the last to a Mr Castlemount, and ended up living alone in a sea-front flat in a magnificent white Art Deco block, Embassy Court, overlooking the sea front in Hove. My sister and I used to visit her occasionally. And I remember during one of these visits, she told me she had wasted her entire life because there was only one man she really wanted to marry, but he was the wrong religion, so both her parents and his parents objected to the union. I felt sad that religious prejudices had ruined her hopes of happiness. Her advice to me was; follow your heart rather than the demands of your parents.

I was always convinced that Aunt Sadie had modelled herself on Mae West, or perhaps Sophie

My Aunt, Sadie Castlemount.
(by kind permission of the Ostrer Family Archive)

Tucker. Not only was the resemblance of her appearance (clothes and hair) and voice uncanny, but also the furniture and decoration in her apartment was almost identical to photos I had seen of Mae West at home in her flat in Beverly Hills or wherever she lived. I liked the idea that Sadie had adopted a film star as her role model, and so became a celebrity by default in her own mind, with a facade to live up to. And why not.

Mae West (the original) also lived in a block of flats, though I believe she owned the building. An acquaintance of mine was visiting tinseltown some years ago. He was very attractive looking and quintessentially English in demeanour (thank God this computer can spell, because I can't), and he had the gift of the gab with an abundance of charm such that he could talk anyone into anything.

He decided to do a "Sunset Boulevard" on Miss West, for which he borrowed and hired a selection of cameras and other photographic equipment. He believed a clump of three or four cameras dangling from his neck would add an air of professionalism to his appearance.

He knocked at Mae West's door with two accomplices (probably out-of-work actors) carrying a selection of tripods and large light reflectors. The maid opened the door (possibly "peel me a grape" Beulah) and "the photographer" announced that they had come to do the pictures. What pictures, the flustered maid asked, blocking their entry. At this point the star appeared on a distant balcony overlooking the entrance hall, and she joined in the negotiation. "The photographer" came clean, explaining that they had gone to so much trouble bringing the equipment. Eventually, with loads of flattery, he talked her into the photo session. No doubt he had to wait a few hours while Miss West was preparing herself for the occasion.

Uncle David was the eldest of the Ostrer brothers. In the late 1940s, when I was a young teenager, he wasn't my favourite uncle because at the time I was too sensitive to handle his biting sarcastic remarks. I still recall him telling me that I had "duck's disease", which he explained meant the ratio between my body and legs was such that I had a tall body propelled by short legs and waddled like a duck. As a result of this revelation I spent hours examining myself and my gait in the mirror, teetering on the edge of a self-conscious depression. On reflection I believe the length of my jacket made my legs appear shorter than they in fact were. Of course, then I was a skinny youth, whereas nowadays with a pronounced belly my bodily proportions are such that no one notices the legs, and I still waddle about like a duck, but don't give a damn.

Years later, David became my favourite uncle because he and his second wife, Inga (Ingeborg),

My Uncle, David Ostrer, and Aunt Inga in 1946.
(by permission of Keystone/Hulton Archive/ Getty Images)

were such a fascinating couple and so devoted to each other. His first wife died in the early 1930s, and he married Baroness Ingeborg Wilmans Edle von Wildenkrow in 1935. They loved art and artists, and the impressionist paintings in their flat at 37 Grosvenor Square were not bought from art dealers but were acquired years earlier from the artists themselves, before they became well known. One small picture, beautifully framed behind glass, was a Rouault painted on a piece of unused toilet paper. Well, I assumed it was unused.

Aunt Inga was from Austria, and spoke English with a German accent. I was convinced she had modelled herself to look like Marlene Dietrich, because the resemblance was striking. Yet, she was so fashionable and up-to-date and outrageously camp. In 1968, shortly before she died I remember going shopping with her to Liberties when she was 68 years old. She was wearing a navy blue PVC

Aunt Inga in 1935. David Ostrer's second wife.
(by kind permission of the Ostrer Family Archive)

plastic mini-skirt, and had a long cigarette holder that would have burnt out your eye if you got in the way. A shop assistant approached and said: "Excuse me Madam, smoking is not permitted". Inga replied: "Don't be ridiculous" and walked off puffing smoke around the shop for the remainder of her visit.

Always when I saw David and Inga walking down the street together, they were arm-in-arm, a devoted couple after thirty years of marriage. But my father, Maurice, loathed Aunt Inga, and told me when his older brother, David, met her, she was wearing a long fur coat with nothing on underneath. Wonder what he would have thought if she had been wearing only a fur wrap around her neck.

David had a reputation for being argumentative, but I didn't find him to be. I found him very laid back and pleasant. He once told me that he was a snob, and felt himself to be a few notches above the riff-raff. I can appreciate his sentiment, when dabbling in the gutter (which one does from time to time), I myself feel a detached superiority.

Uncle David and Aunt Sadie at Hills End in 1965.
(by kind permission of the Ostrer Family Archive)

One year before David died I spent a few weeks holiday with him and Inga in southern Spain, where they used to go every summer. The three of us were walking by the beach one evening, when David said to me that this was the last year he would be vacationing in Spain. Instinctively I knew he was telling me that he was dying, and it felt a bit freaky and surreal because no one had ever told me anything like that before, I was suddenly confronted with the stark reality that life is terminal. I asked what would happen to Inga because I couldn't imagine them apart or her surviving alone. He said she would be following him, which I immediately interpreted as a suicide pact. And I was deeply touched and moved that they had chosen to share this confidence with me. A few months after David died my mother invited Inga to stay the week-end so she would not be alone on her birthday, but she declined the invitation and died on her birthday from an overdose. Though incredibly sad, I remember thinking how beautiful this was, ending her life to rejoin her soul-mate.

Chapter 4: BERTIE & MARK

My cousin Bertram Ostrer, known as Bertie, was Uncle David's son from his first marriage. He looked a bit like a bullfrog with heavy jowls that flapped as he spoke. He went to Oxford, and apart from me, was the only second generation Ostrer who went to university. Bertie hated his step-mother, Inga, who was his father's second wife. During the war Bertie was drinking in the 400 Club in Leicester Square. He was somewhat pissed, and contacted the police, telling them Inga was a German spy, which they had to investigate, even though Inga was in fact from Austria.

Inga died three months after David, and I remember with revulsion that Bertie and my father's chauffeur,

Johnny Isaacs, descended on David and Inga's home at 37 Grosvenor Square, like a pair of vultures pawing over her treasured possessions, before the funeral, before her body had been laid to rest. Small consolation that they at least had the decency to wait until she was dead before they stuffed her jewellery and furs and anything of value into pillowcases.

Nevertheless, everyone liked Bertie because he was amusing and friendly, and the Oxford accent he sported had an authoritative air.

I remember when cousin Bertie crashed his Bentley by driving it over the top of a roundabout rather than around it, which he would have done if he had been sober. Needless to add, this occurred before they introduced the breathalyser. I suspect he was a heavy drinker.

He followed in my father's footsteps and produced ten films after the demise of Gaumont British. The best known was probably Captain Nemo and the Underwater City (1969).

He produced three films jointly with Albert Fennell, who had also worked for my father. Park Plaza 605 (1953) featuring Sid James. The Green Scarf (1954) featuring Michael Redgrave. And, The March Hare (1956) featuring Wilfred Hyde-White. I met Albert Fennell in a petrol station near Gerrards Cross in 1969 after he had produced The Avengers (TV series), which I loved.

Bertie produced the next seven films on his own. The Silent Enemy (1958) featuring Lawrence Harvey and Sid James. Friends and Neighbours (1959) featuring Arthur Askey. I am not an Askey fan. Dentist in the Chair (1960) featuring Bob Monkhouse Nearly a Nasty Accident (1961) featuring Jimmy Edwards. Dentist on the Job (1961) featuring Bob Monkhouse. Mystery Submarine (1963) starring James Robertson Justice. And Bertie's last film,

Captain Nemo and the Underwater City (1969) featuring Robert Ryan and Chuck Connors.

Isidore was head of the clan. He, with two of his brothers, Mark and Maurice ruled the roost I feel Uncle Isidore's attitude toward his other two brothers, David and Harry, and his sister, Sadie, was to largely ignore them. I don't believe he spoke to them, or saw them, for years. He gave them unimportant jobs and an office in Gaumont British, like throwing them a few scraps to keep them off the bread-line. Whereas Mark and Maurice had substantial shareholdings in the Metropolis & Bradford Trust, which controlled Gaumont British, David, Harry and Sadie had no shares in the trust at all. Isidore's shareholding was very much larger than that of his brothers, Mark and Maurice, so he was firmly in the driving seat. However, Maurice was definitely friendly toward the three outcastes.

I remember being invited with my elder brother,

Darryl, to dinner in Montego Bay in Jamaica in the 1950s, the big three, Isidore, Mark and Maurice were there (without their wives), but had not invited David, Harry or Sadie to join them on their holiday.

I didn't know Harry very well, and only ever had a few brief conversations with him, and was never invited to visit his home in Hove. I thought of him as an amiable and very caring person, but somewhat boring with zero charisma. Had I been Isidore, I too would have buried Harry in the script department and forgotten about him.

Aunt Sadie (Isidore's sister) never stopped talking, and more often than not, about herself. I can imagine Isidore finding her incessant chatter headache-making. Whereas I enjoyed listening to her, in small infrequent doses, because I was always gathering material for this book, long before I thought about writing it.

My Uncle, Mark Ostrer.
(by kind permission of the Ostrer Family Archive)

Mark Ostrer's house in Portland Place, London.
(by kind permission of the Ostrer Family Archive)

I suspect there might have been a generation rivalry between Isidore and his older brother, David. You would expect the oldest to be head of the family, but David was not, because he depended on Isidore's patronage. David, my favourite uncle, was not motivated to accumulate personal wealth. He had impeccable taste and enormous style, and lived very comfortably, without a car or extra trappings. He spent everything, and died penniless.

Next I explore the three Ostrers who developed and to some extent ran Gaumont British. My Uncle Mark died in 1958, seventeen years earlier than his brothers, Maurice and Isidore. And so I did not know him as well. He was an extravert, a bon viveur who loved entertaining in his large country house set in 50 acres; King's Beeches, in Sunninghill, Berkshire. I remember the long driveway, which seemed like miles. And the set of lovely Great Dane dogs. Mark was a member of the prestigious Portland where he

The lawn of Mark Ostrer's country house
Kings Beeches in Sunninghill, Berkshire.
(by kind permission of the Ostrer Family Archive)

played bridge. Everyone liked Mark. No one had a bad thing to say about him.

Uncle Mark's second wife, Olive, loved planning dinner parties which she hosted extremely well. She told my sister that Isidore came to stay for a

**Mark and Olive Ostrer entertaining on the patio
at Kings Beeches in Sunninghill, Berkshire.**
(by kind permission of the Ostrer Family Archive)

weekend, and remained for six months. With his reclusive tendencies he spent a great deal of time in his room. But, on one occasion Uncle Mark and Aunt Olive were giving a formal dinner party with the seating placement of the guests carefully prepared by Olive. Halfway through the dinner, the door opened and Isidore, dressed casually, slid into the

**My Aunt, Olive Ostrer with dogs at
Kings Beeches in Sunninghill, Berkshire.**
(by kind permission of the Ostrer Family Archive)

dining room. The guests had to shuffle up to make room for Isidore at the table, which ruined Olive's careful seating plan. And then he said he didn't really want the food on offer, so the cook had to prepare a dish specially for him. Olive was livid, because her dinner party had been ruined. She could easily have hit him over the head with a Champagne bottle, but fortunately she exercised restraint.

One of Uncle Mark's neighbours was the Maharaja of Morvi, and apparently, one day he decided he wanted to perform a surgical operation without any medical qualifications. Fortunately he was not permitted to indulge his wishes at a hospital in England. So he had to wait until he visited India and chop up one of his own subjects. Hopefully British royalty have never had such inclinations, except there was a question mark over the identity of Jack the Ripper.

After Uncle Mark died his house, Kings Beeches, was sold to the Maharaja of Jaipur. Uncle Mark's son, my cousin Edward, told me he visited King's Beeches about forty-plus years after living there. On an outing in the country he drove up the long driveway, everything was derelict and to his horror he discovered the house had vanished as well as a long brick wall. Completely disappeared. There were several dilapidated caravans parked in the grounds occupied by hippy-looking squatters. He made a hasty retreat. He assumed the large house and long wall had been pulled down so that the old bricks could be sold. Similarly, I visited Hills End thirty years after Maurice and Isidore lived there. I peered over the gate, and it looked derelict and unkempt as if no one was living there. I suppose one cannot just turn the clock back and visit the past and expect everything to be as it was. One has to suffice with memories.

Chapter 5: MAURICE & RENEE

The next member of the family to be scrutinised is Maurice, my father. In the late 1920s and the 1930s Uncle Mark had a large house at 80 Portland Place and Maurice (my father) lived in the Mews house behind, as his bachelor pad before he was married. The main house and the mews house were joined so that you could walk from one to the other without going out into the street. At the time, Maurice drove a racy red Buick convertible with a bulb horn that sported a long chrome pipe ending in a snake's head. You probably cannot visualise what I am talking about, but flashy American motorcars looked like that in the early 1930s. Maurice was a very good golfer, and won a lot of trophies. He also loved horseracing and at one time owned several

My father, Maurice Ostrer, as a young man.
(by kind permission of the Ostrer Family Archive)

racehorses. What was he like? He had a serious
disposition and when asked a question would look at
you gravely with a poker face before answering. He

had a sense of humour, was gregarious and enjoyed going out.

My mother, Renee, was born in Italy. She was the first person to appear nude in a play on the London stage in 1927 (A Portrait of Juliette). The play was about a sculptress and Renee was her model. In those days there were strict regulations under which a nude actress was not permitted to move, and only female members of the cast were allowed on stage. This stage appearance launched her career, and the following year she was under contract to the Gaumont British Picture Corporation, appearing in eleven films, under her maiden name, Renee Clama.

Adventurous Youth (1928), Taxi for Two (1929), The Devil's Maze (1929), Greek Street (1930), Symphony in Two Flats (1930) with Ivor Novello (directed by Michael Balcon), The Great Game (1930) with Rex Harrison, The Stronger Sex (1931)

My mother, Renee Clama,
under contract to Gaumont British 1928 to 1932.
(by kind permission of the Ostrer Family Archive)

with Gordon Harker and Elsa Lanchester (directed by Michael Balcon), The Sport of Kings (1931) with Gordon Harker (directed by Michael Balcon and Victor Saville), No Lady (1931, reissued 1943) with Lupino Lane, Never Trouble Trouble (1931) with Lupino Lane, and The Man They Could Not Arrest (1931) with Gordon Harker (directed by Michael Balcon). She gave up her film career when she got married.

Renee loved animals (especially dogs) but disliked horses. She told me she was filming in Deauville, and had to sit on a horse, which suddenly took off. A young actor in the film galloped after Renee and stopped her horse. Understandably she dismounted and decided to walk back. But the actor, having just rescued the heroine, in a display of bravado galloped away and jumped a wall. He didn't make it, fell off and smashed his face, which abruptly ended his career. Renee never had anything to do with horses again.

In the 1930s Maurice and Renee rented a large flat in Grosvenor House in Park Lane, where I was born. In 1934 Renee's father died (my grandfather), and she told me that she had felt his presence after he departed. He particularly liked Lily of the Valley flowers, which have a very strong scent. She said after he died she smelled these flowers in the apartment, even though there were none there. Every night she felt he came to her and lifted her body up, floating it toward the window, which was on the fourth floor. She panicked and used all of her willpower to prevent this from happening, because she feared he wanted to throw her out of the window so that she would join him in death. I can understood how frightening this experience would have been at the time, but assured her he had no malevolent intention. To me it seemed more likely that he just wanted to take her on a brief expedition to reassure her he is doing okay in the afterlife.

Renee told me that in the early 1930s Maurice

chartered a largish yacht for them to sail around the Isle of Wight.   Maurice and the skipper were engrossed in conversation about nautical matters, when Renee asked: "Why is that large Ferryboat heading straight for us?" The skipper replied: "It is OK. We have the right of way." Renee asked: "Does the Captain of the Ferryboat know that we have the right of way?" An answer to this question was not necessary, because the Ferryboat rammed the yacht, which limped into port.

Some years later, Maurice chartered an aeroplane for Renee, himself and friends to fly back to England from Deauville in northern France. Maurice and the pilot were sitting in the front.   While they were crossing the Channel, Renee focused on one dial amongst the large selection of instruments on the dashboard. She leaned over and pointed at the instrument in question and asked what it is for. The pilot said It is the fuel gauge. Renee asked Why

Maurice and family on the beach at Deauville.
(by kind permission of the Ostrer Family Archive)

does it say empty. Maurice and the pilot briefly conferred. The plane turned round and flew back to France, where it refuelled before setting out again for England. It must be reassuring to know that one's life is in such competent hands.

Maurice also owned a house called Ladymead in

West Strand, West Wittering by the sea, but at the beginning of the Second World War the house was commandeered in case of German invasion across the Channel, so Maurice bought a house (called the Dower House) in Chalfont St Peters in Buckinghamshire, where we spent the war years. The Dower House was set back from the road in several acres of densely wooded land, at the top of Gold Hill adjacent to the large common. My brother and I had a model train from Hitchcock's "The Lady Vanishes" which we set up to run round the big kitchen of the Dower House. Another "toy" from the studio was a largish scale model of a Spitfire aeroplane, but I don't know what film it was used in.

Later Maurice moved to a house called Dormers in South Park, Gerrards Cross, where we lived for a short time after the war, until we returned to London to a flat in Grosvenor House, where we remained after my parents had separated. My mother, Renee, lived with us (my brothers and sister) in Grosvenor

House, and my father moved around the corner to 48 Grosvenor Square.

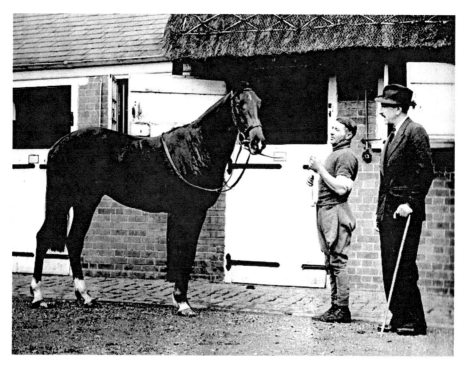

**Maurice visiting his race horse
at the trainer's stable.
(by kind permission of the Ostrer Family Archive)**

In the 1960s, Renee converted a pigeon loft on two acres into her dream house in Denham, where she lived with her mother, my grandmother.

PHOTOGRAPHS ON THIS & THE NEXT PAGE
Renee's mansion: Denham House
in Denham Village, Buckinghamshire
(by kind permission of the Ostrer Family Archive)

In particular, she loved gardening, and in the winter would be pottering in the garden (weeding or something) wearing an ankle-length mink coat, which she didn't like much. I inherited the mink coat. No, not to wear. Originally it cost thousands, was very voluminous and had about a million minks in it (they are only the size of a rat), but at that time no one dared admit they owned a mink coat for fear of being attacked. No one except me. I disassembled it and converted it into an exotic bedspread with a fringe of prairie wolf fur. A bit outrageous no doubt, but the moths loved it. They were swarming in my bedroom like locusts. At the time, moths were about the only visitors in my bedroom.

Though not a part of the Ostrer family history, I feel a brief mention of my grandmother (my mother's mother) adds a flavour of the pioneering times in which she lived. She was born in Builth Wells in Wales in 1880. As a child she was brought to London

**My grandmother, Jessie Clama taking a dip in the sea
with my Aunt Elvira, and mother, Renee.**
(by kind permission of the Ostrer Family Archive)

to watch Queen Victoria's jubilee procession. As a
young adult she supported the suffragettes. Her
husband, Alessandro (my grandfather), was born in

Verona, northern Italy in 1872. They met in a railway carriage. He kissed her hand, and she thought: "How romantic, Englishmen don't do this sort of thing."

They, Alessandro and my grandmother, Jessie, lived in Italy for a while, and later moved into a house in Willesden, north London, where they lived with their two daughters (my mother and Aunt Elvira), plus an English bulldog and a rabbit that used to run around the house. Alessandro was so attached to the bulldog that when it died he had it stuffed by a taxidermist, thereafter it stood on the drawing room carpet frozen in time.

Alessandro died in 1934 at the age of 62, and my grandmother died 45 years later, in 1980, just after her 100th birthday. I was told Alessandro tripped over the rabbit and never completely recovered from the fall and died shortly after.

My grandmother, Jessie Clama.
(by kind permission of the Ostrer Family Archive)

I remember my grandmother fell down stairs aged 95, and broke her hip or leg or something. They said she would never walk again, but she was up and about three month's later as if nothing had happened. She was very strong willed.

After the fall it was decided she ought to live in an old people's home. She settled in and took over. Her round table in the restaurant was like the captain's table on an ocean liner. Only residents she approved of were invited to sit at her table. Inevitably her friends disappeared one-by-one in the night, and were replaced at her table. Once she told me how upsetting it was that all of her contemporaries, relatives and friends, had died. But she felt uplifted by the fond memories from her past.

I remember talking to her about life when she was 18 in 1898. There were no motorcars, only horse-drawn carriages. Crossing the road in London must have been like stepping into a cesspit. The smell must have been awful. Of course there was an army of people employed to sweep up the horse manure. No cinemas, no radio, no television, no aeroplanes. The changes she lived through in her lifetime must have been extraordinary.

Henry, was a large blue Great Dane dog that my mother rescued. He was owned by a publican whose wife didn't like Henry. The ultimatum was, either Henry goes or the wife goes. And Henry went. Henry loved cars, and when he saw an open car door, he would hop in and sit on the seat. If a visitor left his car door open a moment too long, Henry would be inside and ready to go, and it wasn't easy to get him out of the car. One evening we (Renee, grandma and myself) were in one of the drawing rooms watching television, and Henry was laid out asleep in front of the fireplace. The door was always left open, and led onto a small vestibule with a round table, on which was Renee's handbag. A burglar entered through a small window that Renee had left

ajar.   He rifled the handbag, whilst Henry slept
through the whole proceedings.   Not the ideal guard
dog.

Chapter 6: MAURICE

Maurice was the Producer of five films. Band Wagon (1940), Girl in the News (1941), The Young Mr Pitt (1942), King Arthur was a Gentleman (1942), and Time Flies (1944). He was the Executive in charge of Production of eight films. Inspector Hornleigh on Holiday (1939), For Freedom (1940), Night Train to Munich (1940) directed by Carol Reed, Charley's Big-Hearted Aunt (1940), The Man in Grey (1943), Bees in Paradise (1944), 2,000 Women (1944), Love Story (1944). And was Executive Producer of eight films. We Die at Dawn (1943), Millions Like Us (1943), Madonna of the Seven Moons (1945), Waterloo Road (1945), A Place of One's Own (1945), They Were Sisters (1945), The Wicked lady (1945), Caravan (1946). It is all in the title (executive

**My father, Maurice Ostrer, in his office
at the Gaumont British studios in Lime Grove.**
(by kind permission of the Ostrer Family Archive)

in charge of production, producer, and executive producer), and most of these films were made after Uncle Isidore had cleared off. It was as if Maurice blossomed after the shadow of his older brother had lifted. Of course, I have no idea what a film producer actually does, apart from having a grumble when the

**The caste and crew of The Wicked Lady
at the Gaumont British studios in Lime Grove.**
(by kind permission of the Ostrer Family Archive)

project goes over budget, which invariably seems to be the case.

The Wicked Lady (featuring Margaret Lockwood, James Mason and Michael Rennie) was a bigger box-office success than any other Gainsborough or Gaumont British film. More bums on seats than

Star Wars. Maurice wanted to make a sequel, but Rank, who controlled Gaumont British at that time, prevented one being made because he found the film too immoral and unacceptable to his religious convictions.

Mind you, in the days of The Wicked Lady, America went into a tizzy over a bit of cleavage, and scenes had to be re-shot for the American market. In contrast, most modern Hollywood films seem to have an obligatory porno scene in which the main characters simulate orgasm; utterly tedious except for those wankers in the back row. Fortunately with DVDs one can fast forward past the gratuitous sex scenes to get back to the storeyline.

I cannot understand why religion is so obsessed about sex. After all if sex were the most important topic, then surely the gospels would have been a sex manual, whereas the subject is not mentioned by Jesus at all. On the other hand, subjects He did emphasise (like loving your enemies and not accumulating personal wealth) are conveniently ignored by many purporting to follow in His footsteps.

For the last twenty plus years of their lives, my father, Maurice, and Uncle Isidore lived together. They shared a country house in Sunningdale, called Hills End, and also rented a flat on the Croisette in Cannes, a couple of buildings away from the Carlton Hotel. They wintered in Cannes and spent the summer at Hills End. The grounds of Hills End backed onto Sunningdale Golf course, so Maurice could nip out of the garden gate for a round of golf if he felt so inclined. He also kept the flat in London at 48 Grosvenor Square, but rarely stayed there, however I lived there for a few years. Prestigious address, with butler and maid included; not a bad pad for my twenties.

At Hills End, they followed Mark's example of a few years earlier, and had four dogs; two Great Danes and two Boxers. The dogs were not allowed inside the house, but roamed the two acre grounds on guard duty, sleeping on a mattress in an outside room with a permanently open door.

Renee's second-hand blue Great Dane, Henry, followed her around from room to room and never barked. So when he was inadvertently shut in a room, he would eat his way through the door. He was slowly destroying her dream house in Denham. In desperation she shipped Henry off to Maurice's house in Sunningdale to join his collection of Great Danes and Boxers. The dogs were taken for early morning walks on the golf course, but unfortunately Henry ate a golf ball, and died.

In the mid-1950s my sister, Iona, was staying at Hills End. Maurice and Iona were invited to lunch at Mark's house, Kings Beeches, about five miles away. Maurice did not want to disturb the chauffeur, and so decided to drive himself. He had not driven since

1932, but insisted it is like riding a bicycle, something one never forgets. Mind you, I haven't ridden a bicycle for forty years, and am sure I have forgotten how to. Anyway, Iona recalled the experience in which Maurice managed to get into second gear, but couldn't go up to third or down to first. So the entire journey was undertaken in second gear with the engine screaming. Needless to add, on arrival the chauffeur was phoned to collect Maurice and my sister, and the unfortunate car, which required a mechanical overhaul after this expedition.

Often when Maurice was staying in London, we would dine together at his favourite restaurant, the Coq d'Or in Stratton Street. Later the restaurant was bought by Sir Maxwell Joseph, my sister's father-in-law, who further expanded his property portfolio by buying the block at 48 Grosvenor Square and the Carlton Hotel in Cannes. Seemed like Maurice's favourite haunts were being gobbled up one by one by Maxwell.

Maxwell used to live with his first wife, Sybil, in a block of flats he owned in St James. One day he cleared off and went to live with his housekeeper, Eileen, who changed her name by deed poll to Lady Joseph. So there were two Lady Josephs around town, one married to Sir Maxwell and the other living with him. The hostess of a cocktail party, being ignorant of the Joseph situation, had invited both of the Lady Josephs. Inadvertently she introduced them to each other, but when they came face-to-face sparks flew.

Everyone was terrified of Sybil. One morning she was laying in bed waiting for breakfast to be brought on a tray. Nothing arrived. Apparently her staff had fled in the night forgoing their wages rather than endure another day of being bossed and abused by her ladyship. This happened several times with different staff. The continual replacement of staff and repayment of fees was the domestic agencies dream and the staff's nightmare. Sybil was very spoilt. She had a bell-push next to her bath to summon a servant while she was bathing, and another bell-push under the carpet in her dining room for her to stamp on when she was ready to be served.

She was hell In restaurants too. On one occasion she had booked a table for two, herself and a girlfriend, and was shown to a small table for two. Whereupon she relocated herself and guest to a larger table for four. The larger table was reserved, but Sybil refused to move when the manager asked her to. The manager refused to serve her and told her never to come back. Interestingly enough, when Sybil was dining with a girlfriend, it was acceptable, but when she caught sight of two men or two women eating together she announced in a stage whisper that they must be gay or lesbian. My sister, Iona, and her husband, Stephen, took his mother, Sybil, out to dinner. A middle-aged friend was dining with his son in the same restaurant. When Sybil saw the couple, she announced, look at that gay man with his toy-boy. Stephen told her that the man was a friend of theirs and his dinner companion was the man's son. Sybil retorted, I don't believe a word of it.

Chapter 7: MORE ABOUT MAURICE

Back to my father, Maurice. During my grand tour of Europe, a two-year adventure in a convertible Citroen, in the 1960s, while visiting Paris I bought a bottle of cognac as a present for my father. I don't even pretend to know anything about wine myself but I believed the French were adequately versed in these matters, probably breast-fed on wine instead of milk. So I asked this shop for something really special, and they came back with a dusty old bottle of cognac covered in cobwebs 1890 something-or-other, so I bought it and on my return to England gave it to my father. The next time I saw him he returned the cognac saying "Isidore said that 1890 something-or-other was a bad year, so give it to your grandmother, she will drink anything." He was referring to my mother's mother. And he was probably right. I do recall she visited me with my younger brother for a weekend whilst I was doing a pre-university course in Dublin. I had a collection of unopened miniatures as sort-of studenty ornaments, after her visit they were all empty. And years later when I was staying at my mother's house in Denham I remember putting a half-empty glass of red wine down on the table, turned away for a second, looked back and it had gone, and my gran was shuffling away holding the now-empty glass muttering "waste not, want not" and "I'll just rinse out this glass for you under the tap." Mind you, she did live to over 100 with all of her faculties intact.

Another present I sent to my father from Canada was an entire Black Diamond cheese, the whole cartwheel which must have weighed half a ton. The shipping alone must have cost more than the cheese. Anyway, I thought he might enjoy this mature sharp cheddar, but I was mistaken. He wrote back saying: "Isidore said the cheese was made from pasteurised milk, so we threw it away." Well, it was the thought that counts, even if it ended up in the dustbin. Of course, he could have written "Thank you for the cheese, it was lovely" and then slung it out without telling me he had done so. Tact was not one of his strong points, and he undoubtedly ruffled more than a few feathers along the way, no doubt leaving behind him a trail of business associates who disliked him.

He was born in the 1890s so he was a bit straight-laced and Victorian at times. I remember in the late 1960s my younger brother was living at my father's flat in Grosvenor Square, and they met on the doorstep, one entering the other leaving the building. My brother was wearing blue denim jeans, and my father, absolutely horrified said "no one dresses like that in town". Chauffeured about with blinkers on I don't believe he noticed that the 1960s had ever happened.

In my opinion he didn't really like films, I don't remember him ever going to a cinema to see one, or watch one on the television. And he didn't like most actors either, thought of them as having loose morals. He was probably right, after a dozen retakes of a steamy sex scene I can well imagine them feeling inspired to perfect the performance off screen.

Maurice never invited film stars to his home, so we did not get to meet any of them. Stewart Granger was probably his favourite actor, with Michael Rennie second. And Phyllis Calvert was his favourite actress, with Margaret Lockwood second. He liked Flannigan and Allen of the Crazy Gang. And he liked Arthur Askey, who I thought was a frightful ham. Maurice loved cowboy books and would have been in seventh heaven if he could produce cowboy films, which of course they didn't make in England at that time (prior to spaghetti westerns).

Isidore appointed Michael Balcon to be general manager of film production at both studios (Lime Grove and Islington). Over the years he did an outstanding job and proved to be perfect for this position. However, Maurice wanted the job for himself and resented Balcon's appointment. Balcon had several years experience making films, whereas Maurice had no such experience at that time. Maurice threw a bit of a tantrum and cleared off to Hollywood taking Renee with him. In those days, the late 1920s, you did not just jump on an aeroplane and arrive the next day, you spent five days on an ocean liner to get to New York and a few more days in a train to get to Los Angeles. And when he got there, the local film-makers were not falling over themselves to offer him a job, so eventually he returned to England with his tail between his legs. To rub salt into his wounds, Renee was offered a film contract while they were in Hollywood, but Maurice did not permit her to accept it. My sister told me that years later in the early 1970s she mentioned Balcon's name and Maurice's eyes closed to a slit and his mouth contorted to one side and he breathed with venom the word "bastard". And so in one word he summarised his 40-year hatred for Balcon and so ended the conversation with my sister.

Renee thought most of the films produced by Balcon were really good, whereas she did not think much of Maurice's films. Some years later my mother was at a premiere of a film produced by Maurice, and afterward a collection of sycophants were hanging around Maurice saying what a great film it was. Renee did not say a word, and someone asked her what she thought of the film, she replied "I don't like costume films." There was complete silence, you could have heard a pin drop.

A description of Maurice would be incomplete without mentioning his chauffeur, Johnny Isaacs, a cockney from the east end of London where we all originated. He usually wore a shabby-looking dark blue pin-striped suit and no cap, so he didn't look like a chauffeur, but more like an owner-driver behind the wheel of the Rolls Royce limousine. There was a glass partition between the driver and rear compartment in the car. The partition was always open so that Johnny could either join in our conversation or listen and report back gossip to Maurice.

On one occasion I visited Maurice's office at 27 Princes Gate, from which he ran Premier Productions, his film production company that only made one film, a box-office flop. I entered his large office on the first floor overlooking Hyde Park. My father, Maurice, looked suitably impressive, as one would expect a movie-mogul, seated behind his huge desk. Johnny, the chauffeur, was slouched in an arm chair. Both Maurice and Johnny were glued to the television set at the side of the room watching a horserace meeting, which was their shared passion. Of course I was not permitted to speak until the event was over, and then only briefly as they got ready to watch the next race.

Every year Maurice had a private box at the Royal Ascot horserace meeting. The procedure was for guests to gather at Hills End, suitably dressed in grey top hat and morning coat, for a nibble of Caviar and tipple of Champagne, and then be chauffeured to the race course nearby. On one occasion my sister's mother-in-law, Lady Joseph, was invited, and she asked my sister, Iona: "Who is that man over there, gorging on large helpings of caviar?" Iona replied: "That is Johnny, the chauffeur." Johnny was dressed in his usual attire, and so stood out from the guests. Lady Joseph retorted: "The chauffeur eating caviar. I have never heard of such a thing." Iona replied: "Johnny always joins in." Needless to add, later on he was mingling with the guests in the private box at Ascot eating lunch with a glass of Champagne in his hand.

Chapter 8: ISIDORE

And now for the big one, Uncle Isidore, leader of the pack, the brain. He was always known as Uncle Mephi, which was an abbreviation of Mephistopheles My father and the chauffeur and everyone called him Mephi, and I suspect Isidore enjoyed his nickname, but I never found out why he was called Mephi. It was suggested that his demeanour appeared somewhat serious and sinister. Though very astute, he was a soft-spoken and refined gentleman by nature, with a love of art and poetry. Whereas in the rough-and-tumble of business he had on occasion to deal with people who were tough and ruthless, who had clawed their way up to the top, trampling over anyone who got in their way. The nickname Mephi presented Isidore as a dark force to be reckoned

My Uncle, Isidore Ostrer.
(by kind permission of the Ostrer Family Archive)

with, and a powerful image to face his antagonists. Those of a superstitious inclination might have thought Mephi was so-named because he had a pact with the Devil. He was also known as "I.O.", particularly by employees and colleagues in business. Whereas ordinary people have two names (a first name and a surname), I suspect very important people don't require a name at all, only their initial.

Isidore married Helene Spear-Morgan in 1914. He was a junior clerk at the time. At this point two different versions of the family history are available. Mine, and that of my cousin, Diana (Remember her? She was Isidore's daughter, sort of). Diana claimed that her mother, Helene, was engaged to the son of a very rich old Scottish family, but dumped him in favour of Isidore, who was a penniless junior clerk at the time. In the Edwardian era there were rigid class barriers, so I do not understand how a woman who had no money and had to work to support herself, managed to jump these barriers and become engaged to a very wealthy upper class man with the approval of his parents. To me the story sounds like a delusion of grandeur. In my opinion, the reality was one penniless working woman, Helene, marrying one penniless working man, Isidore.

A few years later, after Isidore had prospered he moved into a block of flats at 47 Park Street in Mayfair and acquired a large country house (in East Homdon, Broadstairs) with servants, adopting a life style befitting a gentleman of means in the 1920s. His wife, Helene, who had been a Welsh ballroom dancing instructor, understandably did not adjust to being the lady of the manor, waited on hand-and-foot and bored out of her brain. So after her first three or four children she allegedly became a Lady Chatterley and produced two additional children without the help of Isidore. Eventually he became aware of the situation after observing that the latest offspring was

**47 Park Street in Mayfair, the block
of flats where Isidore lived from 1927.**
(by kind permission of the Ostrer Family Archive)

blond-haired and blue-eyed unlike both himself or his wife.

Though I believe Lady Chatterley entertained herself with the gardener, the story goes that Isidore's ballroom dancer had higher aspirations that reportedly included an Italian aristocrat, de Rosso.

**Isidore's daughter, Sheila, with Mark Ostrer and Olive
at Kings Beeches in Sunninghill, Berkshire.**
(by kind permission of the Ostrer Family Archive)

We only discovered the existence of Llewellyn, one of his children, after Isidore and Maurice had both died. Llewellyn was disabled and spent his entire life hidden away in a private institution, though Isidore financially supported his incarceration.

Isidore's eldest daughter was Pamela, born in 1916. Next was Sheila, born in 1918. The son, Vivian, was born in 1919. Diana de Rosso was born in 1921. The youngest son was Anthony, but I don't know when he was born. I met Pamela and Sheila, more about them later. I never met Diana, even though she worked for my sister and her husband for a short time. I did bump into Anthony once on the steps of my father's office at 27 Princes Gate. He was wearing a long camel hair overcoat with huge lapels and a brown trilby and reminded me of George Cole in the St Trinian comedy films. He left me with the impression that he was about to sell me something dodgy.

Isidore divorced his first wife, which was somewhat scandalous because at the time a gentleman did not divorce a lady, but allowed her to divorce him. I suspect she was a bit of a slut because she allegedly spent the Second World War in London entertaining the troops horizontally.

Helene died in the 1970s after falling off the roof of the block of flats in Kensington where she was living. She was in her mid-eighties at the time, and was walking her dog when she went over the edge. I can imagine her tottering along behind her dog at the end of a lead, when the dog takes off in pursuit of a cat or pigeon. In a way history repeats itself. Isidore's mother, my paternal grandmother, died from falling out of a window in a block of flats.

In 1934 Isidore married his second wife, Marjorie, an American who came to England as a dancer in a show. Mephi did seem to like dancers. I was told by Renee (my mother) that Marjorie befriended Isidore's children while she was reeling him in, and as soon as she married Isidore, she demanded that the children live elsewhere. At the time, his daughter, Pamela was 16 years old, and his daughter Sheila was 14. He installed both in a flat in New Cavendish Square on their own.

Isidore and Marjorie lived in a suite at Claridges in Brook Street. My mother and father were also living at Claridges at that time. One day a letter addressed to Mrs M. Ostrer arrived. My mother told me she assumed the letter was to her, being Mrs Maurice Ostrer, whereas in fact it was to Mrs Marjorie Ostrer. My mother opened the letter, which contained a cheque for £100,000 from Isidore to Marjorie (equivalent to £5,000,000 in 2008). Needless to add when my father, who was lurking about, saw the cheque he snatched the letter and cheque and hastily retreated. No doubt fearing he might be asked for a similar cheque, but he wasn't.

While Marjorie and Isidore were living at Claridges, she had two pet canaries. One day she was cropping their talons, when one of the birds collapsed unconscious. She phoned room service for help and they sent up a bottle of brandy. After a few beaks of liquor the bird revived.

Uncle Isidore sold his control of Gaumont British to Rank in 1941, and drove to Marseilles through occupied France, where he boarded a ship to the US. He said his second wife, Marjorie, had TB, and as a do-it-yourself medical treatment, he moved to the dry climate of Arizona. At least, that is my father's version of events. However, in 1941 it looked as if England was going to lose the war, so it occurred to me that Isidore might have cleared off to save his own skin, leaving us behind for the gas ovens of Nazi Germany. I know fuck all about business, but let's face it, you don't get top dollar selling Gaumont British in the first year of a world war when England is about to be invaded.

No doubt you are thinking it is technically not possible to drive across occupied France during World War Two. To begin with, it would require some sort of permission, travel documents, and a million petrol coupons. In fact, Isidore undertook this expedition in 1940, and sold his control of Gaumont British in 1941, after he had arrived in Arizona. His friend, Lord Beaverbrook, was in Churchill's coalition government, so there would have been no difficulty obtaining permissions and travel documents. Isidore's first wife, Helene, had a flat in Menton in the south of France, and he had visited her and their children, several times by car in the 1920s. So he had previous experience of being chauffeured from England to the south of France.

No doubt you are thinking instead of driving across occupied France, why didn't he take a liner from Southampton to New York? The Cunard liners were no longer in service, because they had been refitted as troop ships. Shipping between England and the US was targeted by German submarines, whereas a ship from Marseilles was relatively safe.

Let's face it, Isidore's success in business was a result of taking calculated risks, and facing up to challenges. And being chauffeured across France during the war was a risk and a challenge. He did it, and he survived. In 1940 it looked like we were going to lose the war, so the risk of driving across occupied France seemed a better prospect than ending up in a German concentration camp and being exterminated.

Chapter 9: ISIDORE & MARJORIE

After the war, Isidore and Marjorie lived in Rivonia, a suburb of Johannesburg in South Africa, in a large American ranch-style bungalow with a big garden & swimming pool, and drove an American DeSoto car. Marjorie hated spending money on the house. The drawing room had no furniture at all, and there was only a bed (no chair) in the guest bedroom. My cousin Barbara, Aunt Olive's daughter, was staying for six months. Marjorie took her into Johannesburg to buy a chair for the bedroom. On returning home, she drove into the garage having forgotten that the chair was strapped onto the roof of the car. The chair did not survive, and Barbara was not offered a replacement.

Marjorie enjoyed going on safari trips, but had to abandon a safari because she had only one lung and could not take the kick from the gun. Isidore joined Marjorie on safari, formally dressed in a lounge suit.

They adopted a Greek boy. In my opinion, very sensibly opting a child old enough to walk and conduct a conversation, rather than suffering the disruption of being woken in the night by a smelly un-house-trained baby. However, the boy insisted he wanted to be a train driver when he grew up, which was not what Isidore and Marjorie had in mind, so they sent him back and exchanged him for a girl, Isabella.

Some years later, Isidore returned to England and Marjorie stayed on in South Africa, and they would meet up occasionally in the South of France.

In 1950, Isidore's chauffeur was cleaning the magnificent Rolls Royce Phantom Two that nine years earlier Isidore and Marjorie had driven across France in. The car was parked in the mews opposite the Park Street entrance to Grosvenor House, where I was living at the time. The huge searchlight-looking headlamps were mechanically dipped by the whole thing tilting forward. In place of the running-board, which cars had at that time, a step unfolded when you opened the door. The rear compartment was upholstered in sky-blue silk with matching throw cushions, and all of the metal work inside was gold. Each side of the rear seat was a lighted recessed mirror with brush and comb fittings. I was very impressed by the car, and never saw it again. I fear it was sold shortly afterward, thereafter for the rest of his life he travelled in a 1951 Cadillac.

Sometimes Isidore would fall asleep in the back of his old Cadillac whilst being chauffeured home. On several occasions the car broke down, but on one such incident the car was lifted onto the back of a breakdown lorry, and they left him asleep in the back seat. A while later Isidore woke up, looking out of the window he saw the car was travelling along, but was horrified to discover no driver in the front seat.

Once I sat in his old Cadillac, and once was enough. I found it revolting, like sitting in an ash tray. The headlining was originally grey but saturated in nicotine, it was now brown. Years of cigar smoke had permeated the interior of the car. Fortunately I only sat in the car briefly while it was parked, I did not have the stomach to travel in it. The old Cadillac became so unreliable, and difficult to get parts, that my father bought Isidore a new Cadillac, which he refused to go in.

Some years earlier, Isidore was crossing to New York on an ocean liner. At that time the US authorities insisted that all passengers must have a valid smallpox vaccination, which of course Isidore refused to have. They threatened to dump him on Ellis Island (where they used to process immigrants), even though the accommodation was not ideal for a first class passenger. Isidore was adamant, he was not going to be vaccinated. In the end to get around this impasse they had to contact a friend of a friend in high places to arrange for Isidore to disembark unvaccinated, and as he said, if everyone else in the States has been vaccinated then no one was in any danger of catching smallpox from him.

In the late 1950s Isidore had a suite at Claridges, and on a couple of occasions I had dinner with him and Maurice. Isidore always sat at the same round table in an alcove, and always arranged to have the bulb removed from the light fitting above the table. I was very impressed, having the lighting in a restaurant adjusted and subdued to suit his requirement, even though one had to squint a bit to read the menu, a small price to pay.

In 1962 I had lunch with Isidore, Maurice and Lord Wilmot in the Plaza Hotel in New York, and I remember being fascinated by Isidore's hair. Nowadays people with grey hair who want to look younger have various concoctions they can use to effectively disguise the grey, but back then it was a blue rinse. And on this occasion he must have used too many packets of the stuff, the only hair I've seen that colour was on Dame Edna.

Lord Wilmot was originally a coal miner, later a labour Member of Parliament, and eventually a Minister in Churchill's coalition cabinet during World War Two. And, as retired politicians do, he became a company director; chairman of the board of Illingworth Morris, which was the textile conglomerate built up and controlled by Isidore. At that time to install a peer of the Realm on the board was thought to give a company a bit of class, like window-dressing for the shareholders. Wilmot was very pleasant. The company's head office was in a small old house in Buckingham Gate (Victoria) with a small

My Uncles, Isidore and Mark, with Lord Wilmot
At Kings Beeches in Sunninghill, Berkshire.
(by kind permission of the Ostrer Family Archive)

flat on the top floor where out-of-town executives could stay when visiting London. Maurice told me a few years later that Wilmot was staying in the flat entertaining a lady in bed, when he had a heart attack and dropped dead on the job. The lady concerned was pinned down under this dead weight, until help arrived and removed Wilmot's carcass. The lady was given a more generous payment than she would have received under normal circumstances, and was rapidly pushed out of the door. Wilmot's widow was later informed that he had passed away peacefully in his sleep.

My sister, Iona, used to visit Hills End often while she was at school nearby. On one occasion she was in the library with Isidore, when a man walked past the window. Isidore got very agitated, and believing the man was a burglar, wanted to phone the police. Iona stopped him phoning, saying: "That is the gardener. He has worked here for ten years."

Isidore wrote three books. The Conquest of Gold, Modern Money and Unemployment (an update of the first book), and his poems. He also collected paintings, Canaletto; Reubens, Constable, etc., and did some portraits and still-life paintings himself. In the 1960s I visited the art gallery in Amsterdam and in the shop bought a postcard of one of the paintings,

Isidore and Maurice.
(by kind permission of the Ostrer Family Archive)

a bowl of flowers, that I felt sure Isidore would like.

And every time I visited my father at Hills End, my postcard was on the mantelpiece beside Isidore's armchair, it was the first thing I looked for when I entered the room. And I was always surprised to see my little postcard because I had expected it to have been thrown out years before. Of course most people wouldn't have noticed my little postcard on the mantelpiece, because it was dwarfed by the large Canaletto painting of Venice hanging on the wall above the fireplace.

Hanging amongst the Reubens and Constables at Hills End, there were impressively-framed examples of his own work. He once told me that an art expert had said he would have been one of the great painters if he had pursued such a career. Hence his own works were hung amongst the immortals. His amateurish-looking paintings were far better than anything I could do, but were regarded as a joke by everyone who saw them. In my opinion the art expert in question was in fact massaging Isidore's ego whilst selling him expensive works of art. Such is the power of flattery.

My claim to fame is that I once helped Picasso inadvertently. In the late 1950s I purchased one of his lesser works (a portrait) which I liked, except for the ghastly background. I was convinced he had made a mistake, and so got out a paintbrush and rectified the situation. Though I probably reduced the value of the work to zero, I can at least enjoy looking at it. Mind you, invariably the artist's signature is worth more than the painting, and Picasso's signature is still in tact.

Isidore was somewhat reclusive, in fact in all the years when my brothers, sister and myself visited our father at Hills End, Isidore would be hiding in his room. And, we only caught a fleeting glimpse of him on no more than a handful of occasions. Of course his presence was felt as we were told: "You can't sit there, that's Uncle's chair".

What I remember about Isidore more than anything, was his attitude toward food. He believed; You are what you eat. A sentiment with which I entirely concur. When I was at McGill University in Montreal, I had a request to buy 25 copies of a book by a Vermont doctor on honey and cider vinegar, which Isidore wanted to send to his friends. Fifty years on, I still use cider vinegar every day. From time to time while staying in Cannes, after a stint of healthy eating he would go for a walk in search of a cream cake, and would go from shop to shop until he found a particular cream cake. When I go through a similar ritual myself, I have to buy two cakes because my dog expects one of them.

On one occasion isidore's food fad was carrots, and he had the staff at Hills End preparing freshly juiced carrots everyday, until he looked in the mirror and noticed his skin had turned a shade of orange, after which carrot juice was off his menu. Another time it was bananas, and when I visited for lunch I noticed a very large silver tray on the sideboard in the dining room piled high with a mountain of rotting bananas, well past their sale-by date. Next time I visited there wasn't a banana in sight.

The case of baked beans. Isidore was travelling about a bit: America, the flat in Cannes, Marjorie's house in South Africa, etc.. He had made arrangements for cases of baked beans to be purchased from Fortnum & Mason or Harrods and to be shipped to the various destinations on his excursion. But they arrived after he had gone. The beans arrived at each port of call after he had left and moved on to his next location. Just as well, otherwise he may have farted his way around the world.

This reminds me of my own encounter with baked beans. Forty years ago, in the early 1970s, I felt World War Three was imminent. So I decided to stockpile a few provisions for such an eventuality. Being a part-time vegetarian, I bought a number of

Isidore and Maurice crossing the Atlantic in 1937.
(by kind permission of the Ostrer Family Archive)

cases of catering-size tins of baked beans from a wholesaler, dug up the floorboards in my small house in Earl's Court and stored the emergency supply of baked beans under the floor. I opened one of the huge tins and ate baked beans for breakfast, lunch and dinner for a week or two. I couldn't face a baked bean again for a couple of years. Ten years later I sold the house and moved away leaving the tins under the floor. I wonder if the baked beans are still in situ.

Though Maurice was Isidore's biggest fan, he didn't always agree with everything. I remember in the early 1970s Isidore suffered from an illness that resulted in his ankles swelling up, and as expected he refused to consult a doctor but instead set about treating the ailment himself by starving himself to remove toxins and only eating selected healthy food. It took 18 months before the swollen ankles shrank to their normal size. A year of two later, Maurice had the same complaint, swollen ankles, his doctor gave him some medication and he was cured in a week or so. So, Isidore's way was do-it-yourself and suffer for 18 months, and Maurice's way was let the doctor sort it out and enjoy the 18 months without discomfort.

Isidore in the 1960s.
(by kind permission of the Ostrer Family Archive)

Chapter 10: PAMELA

Pamela (Isidore's daughter) appeared in the film Jew Suss in 1934. She was 16 at the time, and after watching her small supporting role in this film, I concluded that she had no talent whatever. In this film I felt her pathetic effort largely amounted to posing, talking in a shrill voice, and moaning. I assume she only got the part because her daddy owned the film company. Years later when I eventually met her, I could not differentiate between her over-acting on-screen and her over-acting off-screen. Whilst making this film she became romantically entangled with the cameraman's assistant, Kellino, who she later married. He was rather dishy, so she did have taste if little else.

Jew Suss had two excellent film stars on board, Conrad Veidt and Cedric Hardwicke. I watched Veidt in a silent film he starred in in 1919, and his performance was as magnetic then as in his talkies of the 1930s, and of course later in Casablanca with Bogie. Veidt's contribution to Jew Suss was excellent as expected, but the storyline was so confusing that I have no idea what the film was about. Everyone was rushing about, waving their arms and looking terribly serious, about what I have no idea. I wonder if Uncle Harry had anything to do with the script.

What fascinated me more than anything about the film, Jew Suss, were the sets and props. They were atrocious. Windows and mantelpieces of room interiors, were just painted without relief plasterwork, and so amateurishly that I could have done better myself. And I cannot paint at all. The exaggerated perspective looked like everyone was walking up or down a steep incline. In my opinion the sets were probably painted by an apprentice during his lunch break. The horse-drawn carriages had big chunky wheels that looked-like they belonged on a farm wagon, no doubt left-overs from an agricultural film.

In 1939 she appeared with James Mason (under her married name, Pamela Kellino) in an independent film, "I Met A Murderer". And in 1945 was with James in the Gainsborough film "They Were Sisters". She divorced Kellino, married Mason, and moved to Beverly Hills. In 1951 they were both in the film "Pandora And The Flying Dutchman". The rest of her career, a few supporting roles in undistinguished films and her appearances on American television, are not relevant to this book.

The first time I came up against Pamela was in the 1950s. I was in Toronto and my father wrote to me saying I must contact her because James Mason was in a play in the vicinity. I was in my early 20s and Pamela was older than my mother, so I was somewhat hesitant about meeting her, but I phoned on a Monday. No doubt she had received a similar letter from my father (her Uncle), so she obviously expected my phone call and invited me to come to dinner on Friday, and asked me to phone back Friday morning. When I phoned on the Friday, I was told Mr and Mrs Mason had returned to California on the Tuesday. In other words, when I phoned on the Monday, Pamela was busy packing her suitcase preparing to depart the next day, and she invited me to this fictional dinner as a brush off. My feelings at the time were: "What a stuck-up bitch".

The next time I came across Pamela was watching a game show on American television. The contestants were minor celebrities, though I personally had never heard of any of them. Half way through the show it was quite clear that Pamela was losing, and she accused the winning contestant of cheating, and persistently repeated this accusation for the remainder of the program. I felt I was watching a spoilt brat throwing a tantrum, and cringed at the realisation that I was related to this person, whose behaviour I found so obnoxious. She continually interrupted people while they were talking, and I got the impression she was in love with the sound of her own voice, which may be why someone in Hollywood suggested that Pamela had been vaccinated with a gramophone needle.

Pamela's house in Beverly Hills was originally owned by Buster Keaton. Pamela told my sister, Iona, that when Isidore (Pamela's father) visited California, he was invited to dinner at her home, but refused to eat the food she had prepared so she went into the kitchen, heated some cat food in a casserole dish and served it to him. Isidore ate it and loved it.

Iona, and her husband, Stephen, were visiting California, and went out to dinner with Pamela and Zsa Zsa Gabor, who they said was lots of fun, if you are not a policeman. They collected Pamela from her house, but, Iona told me, when the front door opened they were overwhelmed by the stench of ammonia from the large collection of cats within. No, I am not referring to Pamela herself, I wouldn't be so rude. Finding the smell absolutely disgusting and impossible to breath, they declined to come in for a pre-dinner drink.

This incident reminded me of my experience with a cat lover. I like cats, and had two for many years; two, not thirty five. A retired prostitute lived in a one-bedroom flat around the corner from me in Chiswick. She had thirty five cats. You could see them climbing up the curtains when walking by. At that time, I had an old garage, which I later rebuilt, and I used to park my car off the road up against the garage door. The door had a four inch hole in it, which the aforementioned cat woman enlarged, shoving a pregnant cat through the hole to breed in my garage. An army of old ladies appeared putting opened tins of cat food on the bonnet of my car, and every cat for miles around came to dine, their claws scratching my car's bonnet. When I saw it happening, I approached the old ladies and told them they were trespassing and told them to stop feeding the cats. Of course they didn't stop. Next, neighbours knocked at my door saying the cat invasion was an infestation of vermin, and if I didn't do something about it, they would call the exterminator. Personally I regarded the army of old ladies as an infestation of vermin. Anyway, I knocked at the front door of the cat woman who started the whole thing. When the door opened I was hit by the smell of ammonia and rapidly took two steps back and tried to hold my breath before being asphyxiated. She said she had put the pregnant cat in my garage because she didn't have anywhere else to put it. I replied the situation was out of control and I am going to board up the hole in the garage door. She said, if I blocked the hole, she will poison my dogs. I thought, this bitch is a real animal lover. Fortunately, my neighbours did phone the exterminator who dealt with the problem, rounded up the cats and no doubt the old ladies too.

My final encounter with Pamela, I actually met her in 1975 at her father's funeral. She and Maurice (my father) were the two executors in Isidore's will, and in the will Maurice was entitled to remain at Hills End for the rest of his life, after all, they had shared this home since the early 1950s. Pamela had other plans, and so she arranged for Maurice to be driven up to London after his brother's funeral, instead of returning to the house he had lived in for so many years. She didn't inform him in advance of her plan, but just shipped him off in the clothes he stood up in and dumped him in a flat in Grosvenor House. She boxed up his belongings and sent them to a storage facility. Very stressful for Maurice, aged 79, to lose his home as well as his closest brother. He died within three months, and Pamela became sole executor of her father's estate.

Wealthy in her own right, Pamela was not a beneficiary in her father's will, so there was no immediate urgency to throw Maurice out and sell the house. The beneficiary was Isabella, Isidore's adopted daughter, then in her twenties, and no match for someone as ruthless as Pamela seemed to be. Isidore's wealth was predominantly in the block of shares through which he controlled Illingworth Morris, the textile empire he had built. Pamela, the executor, was entitled to sell these shares on behalf of Isabella, and she did so at below their market value to an off-shore company, which seemed illogical to me because I would have expected the controlling block of shares to sell for a premium.

I mentioned previously that Isidore's secretary, Miss Holder, worked for him for fifty-two years starting in the Ostrer Brothers Bank, continuing through the Gaumont British and Illingworth Morris years, and then moved into Hills End as caretaker/housekeeper until Isidore's death. When Isidore died he had left her no provision whatsoever, which seems rather remiss of someone so wealthy to such a long-serving loyal employee. Pamela rectified the situation by providing her with a pension. Which was very nice of her.

Some of the outdoor scenes in James Mason's last film were shot in Denham Village, where my mother, Renee, and her sister, Elvira, were living at the time. Elvira approached Mason and asked if he would like to come to tea at Mrs Ostrer's home in the village. He replied: "No thank you, I never want to meet another Ostrer again." An understandable sentiment as I was told Pamela cleaned him out and left him destitute, when they divorced.

Elvira (my Aunt), was a bit strong willed, and looked like and reminded me of Bette Davis in The Nanny, and later in life, The Anniversary but without the eye-patch. My mother, Renee, who retired from the silver screen thirty-five years earlier, and her sister (my

Aunt), Elvira, the two pensioner sisters sharing Renee's large house together had overtones of Davis and Crawford in Whatever Happened To Baby Jane. My mother and Aunt lived in separate wings at opposite ends of the house, so they weren't under each other's feet all day every day. At the time Aunt Elvira had been engaged to Karl for as long as I can remember (at least twenty years). I suspected she was waiting just in case something better turned up, but they did eventually get married. Karl was delightful and a perfect gentleman, immaculately dressed and fastidious. Instead of eyeglasses he wore a monocle which was very impressive and quite fascinating. He had forty pairs of hand-made shoes, but his feet spread with age so he had a toe amputated off each foot rather than replace his collection of shoes. His motorcar was pristine and he would not permit shopping bags in it, so Elvira had to make other arrangements to go to the supermarket. I would have thought a few shopping bags in the boot might have been tolerable.

Being driven by Karl was a memorable experience as he begrudgingly tolerated other road users who he referred to as shopkeepers and proletarian swine. He was an attaché in the Austrian Embassy, accustomed to diplomatic immunity. On one occasion after he retired he was stopped by the police driving at double the speed limit. He ordered the policeman to "Stand at attention while speaking to an officer". They were not amused and removed his driving licence for two years.

Chapter 11: SHEILA, VIVIAN & DIANA

When I met my cousin Sheila (Pamela's younger sister, Isidore's second daughter) in the 1950s whilst she was living in Montego Bay in Jamaica. I found her a very pleasant congenial person with a passion for literature and recall she wrote book reviews at the time. Her Canadian husband, Bill Thompson, told me he had been a lorry driver during prohibition driving booze across the border into the United States. And in the Second World War he was a bomber pilot, attributing his survival to not diving to release his bombs but doing so from a greater height out of range of enemy fire. I wondered if the bombs dropped from such a height at that time hit the intended target, but then they landed in enemy territory, so who cares if they exploded in a field full of cows or on a school, we won the war anyway.

Whilst I was there Sheila and Bill were devastated when their sixteen year old son committed suicide, I understand he was found hanging from a tree naked with his clothes neatly folded on the ground. I feel sure the memory of such a shattering experience remained with Sheila for the rest of her life. In the 1970s my father (Sheila's Uncle) told me that Sheila had turned to religion and became an enthusiastic born-again Christian, which my father thought of as a symptom that she had lost a few of her marbles. The transition of a middle-aged Jewish housewife into a bible bashing Christian was beyond his comprehension, though I myself recall wondering at the time if she had thought of her original birth as a sort of religious miscarriage. Personally I have always held the opinion that devoting one's life to licking God's arse in the hope of profiting from a privileged status in the next world is the ultimate in self-interest.

Vivian (nickname: Kiki) was Pamela's brother (Isidore's son), and when he left school he worked for Messrs. Vanderfelt and Company, a stock broker in the city, following in his father's footsteps. He got commission for the companies that Isidore bought for Gaumont British. But as he didn't have to do any work to get the commission, he only occasionally turned up at his office, until one afternoon he bumped into Uncle Mark in Bond Street. Mark asked Vivian why he wasn't at work. And the cat was out of the bag.

In 1938, when Vivian was 19 years old, he married an American show girl, who was performing in the West End, just like his dad (Isidore) had done a few years earlier. I heard a rumour that he was engaged to one American show girl who went to visit her parents somewhere in the States to break the news of her impending marriage, and she asked her best friend in the show to look after Vivian while she was away. But when she returned she found her friend had married him. Hopefully, such friendship is rare. The new Mrs Ostrer was reported in the newspapers saying: "It wasn't love at first sight. I hardly noticed him the first time we met." To which Vivian replied: "I noticed you, and have noticed nothing else since." Vivian only told his father (Isidore) of the marriage some time after the wedding, and had not introduced his bride to Isidore at the time of the newspaper article.

Some years later, my sister (Iona) met Vivian and his wife when she visited California. They were living in Beverly Hills at the time, and my sister found them both very pleasant. My father mentioned that Vivian had changed his surname from Ostrer to Osborne, and Isodore had disowned him, though no reason was divulged other than a vague mention that he was the black sheep of the family. In hindsight I thought Pamela warranted the title.

And lastly, there was Diana. Yes, the one who

offered the alternative version of the family history. Diana was Pamela's sort-of step sister: same mother, different father. She was an opera singer, and claimed to be a secret agent during the war giving song recitals in the neutral parts of Europe as a cover. My cousin, Edward, as a child was forced to attend one of her recitals at the Wigmore Hall. He told me her singing was competent, but she would never make it to La Scala. Someone else described her performance as like listening to an opera singer with a perforated lung. According to Diana, after one of her recitals a gentleman approached her and said: "Do you remember me?". She replied: "No." And he retorted: "We were married." What else can one say.

My sister, Iona., and her husband, Stephen, owned a restaurant in Chelsea in the 1970s, Bruno One in Park Walk, and employed Diana for a short period as a maitre-d. She told me she gave the job to Diana because she had a bubbly personality with an extravagant imagination. However, in the job, the bubbly went flat and was replaced with a dour expression which frightened away the customers. She had to go. I think she moved to Eastbourne or Clacton or somewhere by the sea, and ran a café, and called herself a restauranteur.

PART TWO

Gaumont British

157

PHOTOGRAPHS ON PREVIOUS TWO PAGES
The Gaumont British studio complex in Lime Grove.
(by kind permission of the Ostrer Family Archive)

Chapter 12: GAUMONT

This part of the book is a personal (and unofficial) biography of my family's involvement in the creation and control of the Gaumont British Picture Corporation Limited. In addition to researching the subject, I have drawn from an extensive family archive covering the entire period. I had to wade through thousands of pages of collected stuff (fortunately in chronological order, more or less) but with a lot of repetition in which the same detail was repeated here and there. Though a lot of the archive was somewhat uninteresting, a number of details added an unexpected and fascinating dimension to the story. So I learnt things I did not know before.

To offer the readers (if there are any) a few

titbits, I found three items extremely interesting. The negotiation with William Fox to merge Gaumont British with 20-Century Fox to create the largest film production and exhibiting company in the world. Uncle Isidore stopped film production altogether and closed down the studio complex for two and a half years in the late 1930s. And the installation of projection television in selected cinemas in the late 1930s.

As the story unfolds very large sums of money change hands. So that the reader can appreciate the huge amounts involved, I have in many instances added in brackets an equivalent sum converted to the 2008 value in pounds sterling. For example: In 1932 the Gaumont British Picture Corporation Limited employed 16,000 people with an annual wages bill of £6,000,000 (equivalent to £300,000,000 in 2008).

The story begins with Leon Ernest Gaumont, who was born in 1864. His parents were in service to the Comte and Comtesse de Beaumont near Paris. Leon's mother was a housekeeper and his father was the livery stable manager. The de Beaumont paid for Leon's education at College Saint Barbe where he was an excellent student. He had to leave school at 16 because his financial help was terminated when his parents lost their jobs. His father was a gambler and had reduced the family to financial difficulties. Leon's granddaughter, Marie Talley, told me that he never talked about his parents, but detested gambling and forbid playing cards in his home.

In his spare time he attended lectures at the Trocadero Observatory on astronomy, physics and mechanical precision. His skills and perseverance were so impressive that he was offered a position at the Ateliers (Studios) Carpentier in 1881 specialising in research and optical instruments. He married Camille Maillard in 1888, which brought a very good dowry including the property at 55 rue de la Villette, which later became Leon's studios.

Leon was very ambitious and he joined Le Comptoir de la Photography, which distributed optical instruments, but did not manufacture them. After two years he became director of The Comptoir, and in 1894 decided to manufacture the instruments he was selling. In 1895 Leon went into partnership with George Demeny, who had perfected the transport mechanism used in film projection.

He began making films in France in 1897, initially to demonstrate the equipment he was selling, and to supply the picture arcade owned by the Lumiere brothers, Louis and Auguste. He expanded the business supplying cine camera-projectors to amateurs and processing the films they shot. Leon opened an English branch in 1898, L. Gaumont & Company, in London with a small office comprising two rooms at 25 Cecil Court off Charing Cross Road with a staff of two, Alfred Claude Bromhead and an office boy. Bromhead was in fact Leon's London representative for his equipment and films. And in the same year, 1898, he established one of the first film production studios in England at Freeman's Cricket Field, Champion Hill, Dulwich, where the first film director was Alfred Collins, a music hall comedian. In the beginning the cameraman and director were the same person, and he probably wrote the script (if they used one) and made the tea as well. In the beginning they did not use artificial lighting, and so filming was out-of-doors to get the maximum light, and the sets were painted cloth backgrounds which flapped in the wind.

Leon Gaumont and A.C. Bromhead were not the only people making films in Britain in 1898. In the same year Cecil M Hepworth made films in the back garden of his small house in Walton-on-Thames using his wife and sons as actors. The kitchen was his laboratory where strips of film hung to dry from pegs in the wall.

In 1902 Leon developed the Chronophone, which was a synchronised wax gramophone disc played in conjunction with the silent film Thus pioneering a talking movie almost 30 years before talkies took over from the silent films. More than 80 such films were made by Gaumont between 1905 and 1908, all of them were directed by Arthur Gilbert, and they were shown in selected London cinemas. Though the selection of cinemas at that time was very limited.

The first continuous performance cinema was opened by Gaumont at Bishopsgate in 1906. The program lasted three-quarters of an hour and included the Olympic Games of 1906 and the San Francisco earthquake. Before 1910 there were no full-length films and no film stars. It took a couple of days to make a film and ten to twenty minutes to show it, and they cost about £5. These one-reel comedies and melodramas were shown in any premises without fire or licensing regulations, and the projector had only one reel from which the film was fed, after which it unwound into a basket on the floor. Specially licensed cinemas began to open, and the public asked for the names of their favourite actors which were thereafter mentioned on the screen in the program. By 1906 L. Gaumont & Company's London premises had moved from the two rooms where it started to a double-front shop, and the original two employees had grown to twenty. The business in England was expanding and so Leon formed a British company, the Gaumont Company, in which he owned the controlling interest, but Alfred Bromhead had a minority shareholding.

In 1906 Leon formed the ELGE company in France with an invested capital of 2.5 million francs, which was a considerable amount at that time. He founded Les Establissements Gaumont for film production,

Les Establissements Gaumont
(by kind permission of Marie Tallay)

distribution and to build cinemas. By 1906 films were no longer sold, but were rented. It was said Leon had a patrician disdain for showfolk and their ilk and would never socialise with them. Gaumont made the first feature-length film at Dulwich in 1913, the Life of Richard Wagner. Silent films were usually accompanied by an improvised piano recital, but in this case the musical agenda was provided by the London Symphony Orchestra. Of course a feature-length film required two projectors for continuity, so

Leon Gaumont
(by kind permission of Marie Tallay)

that when one reel finished in one projector, the next reel would start in the other projector. And the basket on the floor was replaced by a take-up reel.

He also developed the Chronochrome which involved simultaneously projecting three pictures through a coloured screen in green, red, and purple violet to create colour films. Again, years ahead of its time. It was privately demonstrated at the London Pavilion in 1913 and thereafter became a regular feature at several West End cinemas.

Leon established the first automatic film printing works at Lime Grove in Shepherd's Bush in 1912, and he also opened Britain's first purpose-built film production studio at the same location in 1914. The building had a glass roof and side-wall because the electric lighting at that time was not strong enough to shoot indoors using the slow film stock. The first war film ever made showing aeroplane fighting was "shot"

The Gaumont Studio with glass roof in Lime Grove (1914)
(by kind permission of the Ostrer Family Archive)

in the new studio. And in 1915 the Government took over the building and the studio using it for research and propaganda purposes, although film production was allowed to continue part-time.

Chapter 13: GAUMONT BRITISH

The Ostrer brothers were originally stockbrokers and stockjobbers, and became an issuing house and a merchant bank, Messrs Ostrer Bros., 25-31 Moregate, London EC2. They were approached by a stockbroker whose client wanted to buy control of a certain film business owned by a foreigner. This proposition was made to, and turned down by, various other issuing houses. In those days investors avoided the film business which they considered to be too risky. The client was Bromhead, the foreigner was Leon, and the film business was the Gaumont Company of London.

The English Gaumont company was a subsidiary of the original French company until 1922, when my

Uncle, Isidore Ostrer, bought Leon Gaumont's control of the English company for £250,000 (equivalent to £9,000,000 in 2008) and formed The Gaumonts Trust Corporation Limited to hold the controlling shares. Leon wanted to withdraw from this country, so the Ostrer brothers agreed to finance the Bromheads to buy out Leon.

Louis Lumiere and Leon Gaumont
(by kind permission of Marie Tallay)

After Leon had sold his interest in the British Gaumont company, he retired to his mansion, Les Tourelles, at Sainte Maxime-sur-Mer, across the bay from Sainte Tropez in the south of France. In the 1930s many well known people in the arts, cinema and science visited Les Tourelles. However, during world war two the Italian military occupied the mansion and the Germans were active in Vichy

**Leon Gaumont's mansion, Les Tourelles,
at Sainte Maxime-sur-Mer, near Saint Tropez
(by kind permission of Marie Tallay)**

PHOTOGRAPHS ON THIS & THE NEXT PAGE
Leon Gaumont's mansion, Les Tourelles,
at Sainte Maxime-sur-Mer, near Saint Tropez
(by kind permission of Marie Tallay)

France.   During the war there was only a limited supply of food, and Leon's brother Charles died of pneumonia complicated by malnutrition. Leon died in 1946 at Les Tourelles.

Half of the voting shares in the Trust Corporation were held by the Ostrer brothers, and the other half by the two Bromheads (the Colonel and his brother, Reginald) who also both enjoyed a long contract each.   Initially Isidore looked upon the buy-out as a speculative investment and he left the Bromheads to get on with running the company much as they had done before. For the next five years the Ostrers were in the background handling the finance, but disinterested in the management.

America developed its home market during the First World War, and thereafter focused on penetrating overseas markets. By 1927 they supplied about 90 per cent of the films shown in Britain.   In 1926 Germany introduced a 50 per cent quota by which half of the films shown in their country had to be home-grown. England introduced a quota that gradually increased from 7 per cent to 25 per cent over several years. In the first year of the quota a large number of mediocre films were produced but it compelled the employment of all the available national talent and a continuity of experience for actors, directors and technicians.

For financial stability the entire cost of production had to be covered by the home market. The British home market was small, compared to the American which was very much larger. For British films to make a profit in their home market they could not cost more than £15,000 in 1927, compared to profitable American films costing £50,000. This disparity reflected in the quality of films made at that time. The Americans also excelled in showmanship and publicity, and the main magazines read by movie-fans were American publications.

Isidore suddenly realised that Hollywood had a virtual stranglehold on the films shown in Britain. He decided the only way to save the industry was to control the entire process of film making, distribution and cinemas. He saw huge potential for refinancing and expanding the enterprise accordingly, and the Bromheads, who were satisfied with the status quo, reluctantly went alone. After all, with 90 per cent of the market lost, it was only a matter time before the company would be out of business. Lt-Colonel A C Bromhead was an accountant and probably of a more conservative financial disposition than Isidore who sailed close to the wind, borrowing millions to realise his vision.

In 1927, Isidore orchestrated a merger between the Gaumont and Gainsborough production companies, two film rental companies (W & F Films, and Ideal Films) and several cinema chains. This combine was registered in 1927 as the Gaumont British Picture Corporation Limited, with Gainsborough Pictures

(1928) Limited as a production subsidiary. The initial circuit of 187 cinemas had increased to 287 cinemas by 1932, including the London Palladium. And increased to 343 cinemas by 1937. At the time, they were called Kinemas spelled with a "K".

Isidore went through several steps to concentrate the distribution of films. He started by merging the original Gaumont Company with Ideal Films to become the Gaumont Ideal Film Company, which he then merged with W & F Film Service to become Gaumont British Distributors. The new company consolidated the distribution of films from both Lime Grove (Gaumont British) and the Islington studio (Gainsborough). Previously Gaumont Ideal, which had ten branches and 700 employees, and W & F competed against each other, but after they had merged they worked together as one distribution unit.

In 1927 Isidore built an extension to Leon's glass studio, to increase the production facility in

Shepherd's Bush, which complemented the smaller Gainsborough canal-side studio in Islington. The original stage of the 1914 glass-roofed studio together with the two new stages of the 1927 extension had a total floor space of 12,000 square feet. And it was designed so that lighting and scenery could be moved easily between the three stages. There was also a fog dispersal and ventilation system so that production could continue during London's worst weather conditions including the "pea soup" fog season.

For brevity I am referring to the Gaumont British Picture Corporation Limited as Gaumont British or GB.

Charles Moss Woolf and Michael Balcon were an important part of the Gaumont British enterprise.

Charles Moss Woolf
(by kind permission of the Ostrer Family Archive)

Woolf was a successful fur merchant in the City. He was basically cautious and shrewd but would occasionally make a bold speculation. He opened an office (two small rooms) in Frith Street in Soho with the intention of distributing films as a spare-time activity. During the day he focused his attention on furs, and during the evening on films. At the end of his first year he found his turnover from films was more than £130,000, so he decided to take them more seriously. He obtained sole distribution rights for Harold Lloyd's films in Britain. In 1919 Woolf bought half of a minor film company for £250, and launched Gainsborough with Michael Balcon, who had previously started a small company in Birmingham with his brother to rent and distribute films. Due to the flood of cheap American films, British film production was almost wiped out over a three-year period. Woolf mortgaged everything he owned to ride out the invasion, and survived. In 1927 Woolf sold his interests (including W and F

Film Service) to Gaumont British for £500,000 (equivalent to £22,445,000 in 2008).

Michael Balcon
(by kind permission of Jonathan Balcon)

Michael Balcon had been successfully producing films at the Gainsborough studio in Islington from 1924. After the merger with Gaumont British this production facility became Gainsborough Pictures (1928) Limited, and Michael Balcon became chief executive officer of the corporation as well as managing director of Gainsborough Pictures. He was in charge of production of all Gaumont British films, and therefore producer of all Gaumont and Gainsborough pictures. The Gaumont banner was dropped in 1938, and all films produced thereafter until 1950 were under the Gainsborough banner. Incidentally, Uncle Harry's step-daughter, my step-cousin, was the Gainsborough lady, who nodded her head at the beginning of each film. Gainsborough used a nodding relative whereas Metro-Goldwyn-Mayer used a roaring lion. But then I suppose, what else can you do with a spare relative?

The Bromhead brothers (Col A C, the GB chairman, and his brother, Reginald, managing director) were highly respected for their work over the previous 30 years in developing the film industry. But, in 1929 Lt-Colonel A C Bromhead resigned and was replaced by Isidore Ostrer as GB chairman, Mark

PHOTOGRAPH ON THE PREVIOUS PAGE
Alfred Claude Bromhead
(by kind permission of Marie Tallay)

A.C. Bromhead's estate, Douglas House,
in Petersham, Richmond.
(by kind permission of Marie Tallay)

Ostrer became vice-chairman, and Charles Moss Woolf deputy-chairman. Reginald C Bromhead resigned and was replaced by Woolf and William

Evans as joint managing directors. Presumably the corporate pecking order was sustained by concocting tiers of new titles, such as "vice" bla bla and "deputy" bla bla. At that time the positions of President and Vice President were rare in a British corporation. The Managing Director of a British company was equivalent to the President in an American company. In 1930 Isidore created the position of President in Gaumont British which he filled himself and resigned his chairmanship, and in 1932 Lord Lee of Fareham became Vice President of GB.

At the time Isidore was negotiating a merge with William Fox to inject considerable finance into the corporation. This potential merge was blocked by Colonel Bromhead. Isidore was furious, and insisted on the Bromheads resignation from GB and its subsidiaries and associated companies. Previously Isidore had pulled the strings from behind the scenes, now he stepped out from the shadows into the driving seat.

Colonel Bromhead had disposed of Leon Gaumont's control a few years earlier, and was not prepared to accept any future foreign control, so he got the articles of the company amended to deprive foreign investors (like Fox) of a vote and to ensure that only British subjects could be directors of the company. The Bromheads delayed their departure until the articles of the company had been amended to exclude foreign voters, and insisted that the Ostrers buy the 1,316,517 unissued ordinary voting shares of 10 shillings each for 24 shillings and 6 pence per share.

Here is a morsel of number crunching for the fastidious readers, if there are any so inclined. The 1,316,517 shares cost £1,580,000 (equivalent to £68,220,000 in 2008), however Isidore paid 10 shillings per share with a promise to pay the balance by February 1930 (the next year). Thus the Ostrers paid out £658,000 (equivalent to £28,412,000 in 2008).

The Gaumonts Trust Corporation Limited held more than fifty-one per cent of the ordinary voting shares in the Gaumont British Picture Corporation Limited. Messrs Bromhead and Messrs Ostrer Bros were the largest shareholders in the trust, and jointly controlled the corporation, though I suspect Isidore had a slight edge on the situation. The Ostrers bought the entire holding of GB voting shares from the trust corporation, which was then liquidated. By now you are probably wondering, where did all this money come from. The answer is William Fox.

Isidore went to New York and persuaded William Fox to pay £4,000,000 (equivalent to £184,560,000 in 2008) for 49 per cent of the Ostrer's controlling shares.. The Bromheads disagreed with Isidore's strategy, and so the Ostrers paid £600,000 to buy the Bromheads out. (equivalent to £27,680,000 in 2008).

When Isidore closed down The Gaumonts Trust

Corporation Limited he moved control of the Gaumont British Picture Corporation into the Metropolis and Bradford Trust Company, which was a private company that he launched for that purpose. The new Trust held 3,105,000 of the 5,000,000 Gaumont British voting shares, and thus maintained control of GB by a substantial voting majority The stock of the new Trust comprised 1,000,000 "B" non-voting shares, and 10,000 "A" voting shares. 750,000 of the "B" non-voting shares were held by the United American Investing Corporation believed to be acting as nominee for Fox Film, and the remaining 250,000 of the "B" non-voting shares were held by the Ostrer Bros.. 203,333 of these "B" shares were held by Isidore Ostrer, 23,334 by Mark Ostrer, and 23,333 by Maurice Ostrer. Their brothers, David and Harry, had nothing.

Initially 4,750 of the "A" voting shares were held by the Fox Film Corporation (Fox Film) and a further 4,750 "A" voting shares were held by Isidore. The remaining 500 "A" voting shares were held, 100 shares each, by Mark Ostrer, Maurice Ostrer, Ronald Bruce McDonald, Francis Henry Parrott, and Lord Lee of Fareham. McDonald and Parrott represented the Fox interest. So no one individual held outright control, but Lord Lee was the permanent Chairman who held the balancing vote.

Earlier I mentioned that Isidore had bought 1,316,517 unissued voting shares in Gaumont British, and had paid 10 shillings per share with a promise to pay the balance of 14 shillings and 6 pence per share by February 1930 (the next year). In fact he had entered into an agreement with Fox who undertook the liability of the balance of the purchase price on these shares. This undertaking to pay the outstanding calls on the shares was part of Fox buying into the Metropolis and Bradford syndicate. However, after the Wall Street crash, it was uncertain that Fox would be able to pay this call. And If he had not done so, Isidore's control of GB would have been considerably reduced if not lost entirely. In fact AT&T paid, probably with a eye on equipping the Gaumont chain of cinemas. So Isidore was saved and did not share the fate of William Fox.

The Metropolis and Bradford Trust Company, owned control of the Gaumont British Picture Corporation Limited, which in turn owned control of 68 subsidiary companies including Gainsborough Pictures (1928) Limited, Standard Film Company, Provincial Cinematograph Theatres, Denman Picture Houses, Gaumont British Distributors, and G-B Screen Services. There were a further 20 associated companies including Baird Television and Bush Radio.

After the Bromheads departure Isidore and Woolf were summoned to New York to confer with the executives of the Fox Film Corporation regarding a rearrangement of the Gaumont British Picture Corporation. At that time through interlocking groupings Gaumont British had control of three film renting agencies and two film production companies. Fox Film wanted all of these facilities to be run from one centre.

In 1930, Isidore hosted his own personal dinner party for the Prime Minister, Ramsay MacDonald, and the Dominion Premiers who were in London for a conference. I suppose if you invite the Prime Minister to dinner, and he comes, it could be construed that you have made it socially. On the other hand, politicians being politicians, MacDonald might have come in the hope of collecting funds for his party or a directorship for his retirement.

Chapter 14: FOX

At this juncture in the story, I feel it necessary to take an extended diversion to explain exactly who William A Fox was.

Before Fox went into films, he was in low-priced tailoring. He was a strong-willed and somewhat bombastic individual and well known for the strength of his voice with which he could shout anyone down at meetings. He was accustomed to getting his own way. He went into films in Brooklyn in 1904.

Before the Wall Street crash in October 1929 the William Fox Corporation (Fox Corp) was the holding company that controlled the empire he had built with assets worth about $500,000,000, it was the largest film producing, distribution, and theatre company in the world at that time. The holding company controlled the Fox Film Corporation and the Fox Theatres Corporation.

In the summer of 1962 the Polish author Jerzy Kosinski invited me inside the Park Avenue apartment where he lived with his wife, Mary Hayward Weir, the American steel heiress. The interior of the apartment was sumptuous, a large entrance hallway, walls covered in exquisitely grained marble, staircase to the upper floor, and the beautifully panelled library. Of course I was very cool and pretended that I was not impressed by such opulence in order to give the impression that such surroundings were part of my every day life. Whereas in reality I have lived in my share of dumps and seedy rooming houses. In my mind I recalled this magnificent Park Avenue apartment, a few years later when my father, Maurice, was describing

William Fox with starlets in 1920.
(by kind permission of
Bride Lane Library/Popperfoto/ Getty Images)

William Fox's apartment in Park Avenue where he was invited for dinner in late 1928 or early 1929. He said the large entrance hallway inside the apartment had marble walls and a fountain water feature. The dinner service was gold. A bit ostentatious but you unmistakably knew that you were in the presence of a movie mogul.

The Fox Film Corporation was formed in 1915 by William Fox to control his various film production companies, including the Fox Film Company, the First National Pictures Corporation which he sold in November 1929 to Warner Brothers for £2,000,000 (equivalent to £92,280,000 in 2008), and Metro-Goldwyn-Mayer (MGM) which he acquired in August 1929 when he bought control of Loews Incorporated (Loews) who controlled MGM. He paid $108,000,000 for control of Loews and MGM. And Fox paid $50,000,000 for another studio in Hollywood, which included a five-year $100,000,000 production schedule.

During the two years before the Wall Street crash Fox went on a buying spree with borrowed money. Through Loews he got 175 cinemas (67 of them in New York). He also bought a further 200 cinemas in New York and the Poli cinemas in New England for $26,000,000. And he paid $100,000,000 for West Coast Theatres Incorporated.

He had increased his portfolio of cinemas controlled by the Fox Theatres Corporation to 1,200. But it wasn't all easy going for him, because the US Government brought an anti-trust action against Fox to prevent him voting on his Loew's shares which they claimed would reduce competition in interstate commerce.

William Fox borrowed $91,000,000 as a short-term loan in early 1929 to buy into Gaumont British (GB) and Loews. Fox's dilemma was that the controlling shares of Loews unexpectedly came on the market. I believe the principle shareholder died and his widow wanted to sell. She didn't want a film studio and collection of cinemas, she wanted the cash to enjoy without the headaches. Fox couldn't let all those cinemas and MGM slip through his fingers into the hands of a competitor, so he had to get the short-term loan. With annual earnings of $33,000,000 he did not think repaying the loan would be a problem. Then the stock market crashed and everything changed. He was in negative equity because the amount he borrowed (short-term) was more than the post-crash value of the collateral, his Fox shares.

In the Wall Street crash of October 1929 William Fox lost £20,000,000 (equivalent to £922,800,000 in 2008). The talkies had just begun, and Western Electric, a subsidiary of the American Telephone and Telegraph Company (AT&T), made 90 per cent of the world's talking picture equipment at that time, and Fox was described as their best customer, which was not surprising equipping and maintaining his 1,200 cinemas. In December 1929 AT&T held $15,000,000 of short-term notes of the Fox Film Company (Fox Film) due for repayment by April 1930., and Halsey Stuart & Company underwrote $12,000,000 of Fox notes.

Though William Fox remained head of Fox Film in name, a board of trustees was appointed so that the short-term loans could be extended into long-term loans rather than foreclosure. In the immediate aftermath of the Wall Street crash, Fox was not able to get its issued stock underwritten, even though the corporation's annual earnings were $33,000,000.

Fox was unable to meet the short-term note acquiring Gaumont British, but the deposit had already been paid and it was understood the deal would be carried through by AT&T.

Three trustees were appointed to oversee the Fox Corporation, as there were others negotiating to buy some or all of the assets of the Fox companies: William Hearst and Louis B Mayer. Everyone was pecking at poor Mr Fox's bones. Two groupings of banks were competing to refinance the company, AT&T wanted to keep the contract to supply the talking picture equipment in the 1,200 cinemas, and the Fox shareholders wanted the receivers brought in.

In January 1930 a group of Fox shareholders filed receivership suits against Fox proposing a board of trustees and a promise of new financial backing if William Fox agreed to surrender control, which he refused to do. William Fox's lawyer said the Fox companies are solvent and if new trustees are appointed then no reorganising and no new finance was needed.

A new lawsuit was filed against William Fox in the Brooklyn Court requesting him to resell the stock he had bought in August 1929 in Loews Incorporated. The shares were now worth considerably less than he had paid for them before the stock market crash.

Twenty policemen were on guard outside the Fox Film studios where six hundred shareholders of the Fox Film Corporation were at a five-hour meeting that was temporarily adjourned due to unresolved arguments.

Mr Fox personally owned 50,000 "B" voting shares which controlled the Fox Film Corporation, and which had been deposited as collateral for his loan. The plan was to return the 50,000 voting shares to Mr Fox after the debts had been repaid from the money raised by the proposed reorganisation. However, in April 1930 Mr Fox sold his 50,000 "B" voting shares for $20,000,000 and was also paid $500,000 a year for five years as chairman of an advisory committee. The control of Loews (and MGM) now passed to Radio-Keith-Orpheum (RKO), which was affiliated with the Radio Corporation of America (RCA).

In 1932 the Fox Film Corporation issued a writ against Isidore and the Metropolis and Bradford Trust to try and recover the money William Fox had invested. Surely, the first rule of finance is: Don't take a minority holding in a private company and expect to get your money back. Needless to add Fox did not get any of their money back, not a penny, but instead agreed a mutually beneficial arrangement regarding exhibiting each other's films. And in August 1932 the Ostrer brothers signed an agreement with Fox Film which inferred that Gaumont British in some measure came under the influence of Fox despite the condition in the Gaumont British articles that control cannot pass into foreign hands.

In 1934 Gaumont British was very successful and had a surplus of funds. The Loew shares that William Fox had bought in 1929 which gave him control of Loew Theatres and Metro-Goldwyn-Mayer, were for sale again, and they were offered to Gaumont British, but my Uncle Mark, joint Managing Director of GB, declared the Ostrers were not interested. I think that decision was a mistake.

The Fox Film Corporation merged with Twentieth Century Pictures in 1935 to become Twentieth Century-Fox Film Corporation (20th Century Fox), who thereafter held Fox Film's "A" and "B" shares in the Metropolis & Bradford Trust. By 1936 Lord Lee had resigned and relinquished his "A" shares, and the holding of "A" shares had changed so that 20th Century Fox held 4,700 "A" shares, plus 150 shares held by Fox nominees, and 50 shares held by Sidney R Kent, the president of 20th Century Fox. So 20th Century Fox effectively held 4,900 "A" voting shares in Metropolis and Bradford, and the Ostrer brothers, Isidore, Mark & Maurice, jointly held the controlling 5,100 "A" voting shares.

In 1936 Metropolis and Bradford held 2,915,000 of the 5,000,000 Gaumont British voting shares, 2,100,000 of these GB voting shares were held on account for Fox, and 815,000 were held on account for the Ostrer brothers. In other words, Fox had bought Gaumont British but they did not own control of the corporation. Under the circumstances it is not surprising that they objected when the control was offered for sale to other interested parties.

Wow. Both Uncle Isidore and William Fox were so similar in many ways. They both started from nothing, they had the same vision of creating a self-reliant business which controlled the entire process from production, through distribution and cinema ownership. Making films and showing them. They both fuelled their ambition on vast borrowed funds, and both sailed really close to the wind. Let's face it, if you use other people's money, then all you risk losing is other people's money.

If Wall Street had not crashed in October 1929, Fox Film and Gaumont British would have merged, creating a vast empire with 1,600 cinemas and Fox and MGM studios in Hollywood and Gaumont and Gainsborough studios in England.

Chapter 15: CINEMAS

Is anybody there? If you have got this far without being bored to death, you are about to be. I suggest you either skip this section of the book, or pour yourself a large gin-&-tonic and glaze over the next few paragraphs in an alcoholic stupor. By 1937 Gaumont British controlled 343 cinemas, and this part of the story covers how these cinemas became a part of the corporation. Most readers I am sure would be satisfied to know that the cinemas existed, but no doubt there are a few (there always are) who demand every minuscule detail, and this is for them.

The Ostrer triumphs started with the original flotation, after which they acquired control of the General Theatres Corporation which had a capital value of

£1,900,000. Next, Gaumont British bought the Standard Film Company, which controlled the Provincial Cinematograph Theatres circuit of 116 theatres, valued at £3,500,000. Lord Beaverbrook and William Evans were directors. This amalgamation gave Gaumont British over 300 theatres, including most of the West End of London and the main theatres in every big city in the United Kingdom. Evans became a director of GB.

Charles Gulliver and William Evans were joint managing directors of Moss Empires Limited (capital value £1,318,785), but they resigned in 1932 when Gaumont British took control. Lord Beaverbrook sold his interest in Moss Empires to GB for more than £100,000. Remember the Bromheads (Colonel A C and his brother R C) who used to run Gaumont British until Isidore got rid of them? Well they both turned up as directors of Moss Empires until GB bought the company. Another disgruntled ex-director of Gaumont British, William Evans, reappeared as

Joint Managing director of Moss Empires. Evans resigned from GB in 1931, one year earlier, saying he "could not see eye-to-eye with Mr Isidore Ostrer". Presumably after Isidore had bought Moss Empires, he flushed out the three disenchanted ex-directors of GB.

Gulliver had built up a chain of variety theatres, the Gulliver Houses, which included the Palladium in London, but he retired when his theatres were purchased by Loughborough Theatres Limited.

All of the voting shares in the General Theatres Corporation Limited were owned by Gaumont British. But the preference shareholders enjoyed a special voting right when their dividend was more than six months in arrears. Under these circumstances they could outvote the ordinary shareholders. Gulliver and Evans had been buying preference shares for this purpose. This minor attempted coup against Isidore failed because the dividend was paid at the last minute. The delay was not an oversight but was to help the company's cashflow at the expense of the shareholders.

Gaumont British controlled a holding company, Denman Picture Houses, which in turn controlled a large number of cinemas as well as smaller groups of cinemas.

Brothers Phil, Sid & Mick Hyams who were originally bakers in the east end of London, built up the Hyams circuit of London cinemas with a total capacity of 10,000 seats. Gaumont British had arranged a booking deal with Hyams, but the Kinomatograph Renters' Society vetoed the plan and threatened to boycott these cinemas. To counteract this problem in 1935 Gaumont British formed a new subsidiary company called GB Super Cinemas to control these cinemas as well as other properties added later. The Hyams brothers became directors of the new company.

And United Picture Theatres, bla, bla. That is enough about the cinemas. I am boring myself to death and falling asleep at the keyboard, so let's move on and get back to the main story.

Chapter 16: LIME GROVE STUDIOS

The original studio (with the glass roof) opened in Lime Grove in Shepherd's Bush in 1914. An extension of this studio opened in 1927. The entire studios complex was demolished and rebuilt on a much larger scale, opening in 1932. Isidore insisted that only British materials and labour was used for this undertaking to help the economic depression of the early 1930s. Isidore did have a social conscience.

In 1898 the Gaumont company employed one man and an office boy, Thirty years later in 1932 Gaumont British employed 16,000 people with an annual wages bill of £6,000,000 (equivalent to £300,000,000 in 2008).

The new 1932 studio complex in Lime Grove had six large production stages, the largest of which was 85 feet wide and 136 feet long. There was a heated water tank 48 feet long, 18 feet wide and 10 feet deep with underwater lights in the sides for filming underwater scenes. Ships were shot using scaled models in the tank, or actors with modelled sections of ships. I recall seeing the water tank when I visited the studio as a child. It was set up to shoot a naval battle scene, and I remember being impressed how large and detailed the model ships were. The tank was floored over with removable traps that provided access to any part of the tank. The removable traps were covered with wooden blocks that matched the studio floor. The tank could be heated quickly by steam ejectors, that drew cold water from the tank, mixed it with steam and then discharged the heated water back into the tank. The heated water was required for filming scenes in which the actors were submersed in the water, such as shipwrecks and

The Gaumont British studios in Lime Grove.
(by kind permission of the Ostrer Family Archive)

The Gaumont British studios in Lime Grove.
TOP: The roof used for outdoor scenes.
BOTTOM: Stage 4 viewed from gallery.
(by kind permission of the Ostrer Family Archive)

swimming, etc.

The six large production stages were served by three lifts; one passenger and two goods lifts. The latter were capable of taking the largest motor car up to the large flat roof which covered the entire building, and was fitted with the necessary facilities to be used as a stage for shooting outdoor scenes.

There were galleries at two heights around each studio for placing and directing the lighting, and in addition two cross gangways at the ceiling level. The overhead lighting was suspended from trolleys on runways across the ceiling, so that lamps could be concentrated and banked as required. The upper gallery was also served from the lift for transporting the large sun-arcs, which weighed nearly half a ton, and the lower gallery had a trolley system for the quick repositioning of lamps. In the early days of production six lamps were used on the floor, whereas

The Gaumont British studios in Lime Grove.
TOP: Stage 6 viewed from gallery.
BOTTOM LEFT: Stage 5.
BOTTOM RIGHT: View along the gallery.
(by kind permission of the Ostrer Family Archive)

The Gaumont British studios in Lime Grove.
TOP: The 6 Generators.
BOTTOM: Studio Lighting.
(by kind permission of the Ostrer Family Archive)

217

**The Art Department at the
Gaumont British studios in Lime Grove.**
(by kind permission of the Ostrer Family Archive)

Models were used in production.
TOP: close-up of model at bottom.
The Gaumont British studios in Lime Grove.
(by kind permission of the Ostrer Family Archive)

TOP: The Plastering Workshop.
BOTTOM: The Carpentry Workshop.
at the Gaumont British studios in Lime Grove.
(by kind permission of the Ostrer Family Archive)

TOP: The Make Up Department.
BOTTOM: A Star's Dressing Room.
At the Gaumont British studios in Lime Grove.
(by kind permission of the Ostrer Family Archive)

in 1932 over 300 were needed, varying from 500 to 5,000 watts. All of the electrical apparatus for lighting and power was controlled from switchboards on the floor and up in the galleries. The power was supplied by six generators weighing eight tons each.

There was an orchestration theatre, and 49 dressing rooms that could accommodate up to 600 actors. Each of the studios was fed separately from all of the workshops and dressing rooms, so as to avoid disturbing work in adjoining studios. And each studio had its own separate suite of monitoring and recording rooms, positive and negative loading rooms, camera store, drawing offices and art department, paint shop, etc. There was a big underground area for storing properties, filled with Louis Quinze sofas and armchairs, chandeliers etc., like a huge furniture cave full of antiques and reproductions.

TOP: Examining the film.
BOTTOM: Developing Machines.
The Gaumont British studios in Lime Grove.
(by kind permission of the Ostrer Family Archive)

TOP: The Film Drying Cabinets.
BOTTOM: The Film Drying.
The Gaumont British studios in Lime Grove.
(by kind permission of the Ostrer Family Archive)

TOP: Cutting the Film.
BOTTOM: Printing the Film.
The Gaumont British studios in Lime Grove.
(by kind permission of the Ostrer Family Archive)

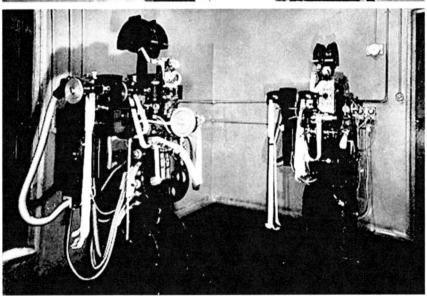

TOP: Sound Monitoring.
BOTTOM: Sound Printing.
The Gaumont British studios in Lime Grove.
(by kind permission of the Ostrer Family Archive)

The new laboratories and the film printing plant handled over two million feet of film a week. There were fifteen cutting rooms, and sixty-two film vaults.

The heating and ventilation to all of the studios was through ducts and grilles concealed in the ceiling space and the system was completely noiseless. The ventilation had a dual purpose. Firstly, to efficiently ventilate the studios and dissipate some of the intense heat from the lighting thus providing more comfortable working-conditions for the actors and production teams. And secondly to filter the air and make the atmosphere perfectly clear and free from dust and fog. It was necessary for the air to be fog-free to get high quality photographic results with sharp rather than hazy images.

This clear atmosphere was obtained by passing all the air through special filters before forcing it by a silent centrifugal fan through the ductwork into the studios. About fourteen tons of air was delivered into the studios hourly, after being filtered and tempered to meet the required conditions.

All of the studios and the adjacent offices were protected by a sprinkler system, with about 3,000 heads, three stop valves and about six miles of pipes. The sprinkler system was fed by two separate water mains, so that there would be a continuous supply of water if one of the mains was turned off for repairs. Full facilities as to emergency escape and inter-communication were provided.

The adjoining block, known as studio No. 2, was originally built for silent films in 1927, and was continually in use, even while the new block was being erected. By 1932 it had been reconstructed for sound film work, forming a studio 116 feet long, 57 feet wide and 33 feet high. The existing roof had been remodelled to take a suspended sound-proof ceiling, and ducted air-ventilation was installed, including fog filtering. But, when the talkies came in, they made the film High Treason before this studio had been fully sound-proofed. For years the glass roof had been a meeting place for local birds, and to prevent their twittering from interfering with the sound-recording, this film had to be shot between midnight and dawn. Making the film at night was possible because the lighting was much brighter than it had been when the glass studio opened fifteen years earlier.

About 100,000 square feet of surface in four studios had been treated with acoustic damping material, nevertheless The most perfect studio soundproofing would, in those days, have been virtually useless if the sounds recording apparatus was not perfect. To this end, the Corporation developed their own sound-recording and reproducing system through British Acoustic, which was a separate subsidiary company, and this system was installed throughout the new studios.

It was proposed to spend £1,000,000 each year to make 40 films a year in total between Lime Grove (Gaumont pictures) and Islington (Gainsborough pictures). Gaumont and Gainsborough made 721 films in which 1,274 actors and actresses appeared, and many of the 88 directors who made these films (including Alfred Hitchcock) started their career in this company or its subsidiaries.

Before Alfred Hitchcock's directing debut, he adapted the screenplays for three Gainsborough films: The Passionate Adventure (1924) and The Prude's Fall (1924), and The Blackguard (1925). He then directed five Gainsborough films: The Lodger (1926), The Mountain Eagle (1926), The Pleasure Garden (1926), and Downhill (1927), and Easy Virtue (1927). After a six year absence, he directed five Gaumont films between 1934 and 1937: The Man Who Knew Too Much (1934), The 39 Steps (1935), starring Robert Donat, Sabotage (1936), The Secret Agent (1936), and Young And Innocent (1937). In 1938 he directed his final film for the corporation, the Gainsborough classic, The Lady Vanishes. Hitchcock was paid £10,000 a year (equivalent to £500,000 in 2008).

This is a list of some of the celebrated actors and actresses who either starred in Gaumont or Gainsborough pictures, or had supporting roles in these films and then went on to achieve fame later in their careers. Peggy Ashcroft, Arthur Askey, Richard Attenborough, Honor Blackman, Claire Bloom, Dirk Bogarde, Phyllis Calvert, Madeleine Carroll, Petula Clark, George Cole, Cecily Courtneidge, Noel Coward, Diana Dors, Bud Flanagan & Chesney Allen, John Gielgud, Stewart Granger, Edmund Gwenn, Irene Handl, Cedric Hardwicke, Rex Harrison, William Hartnell, Jack Hawkins, Will Hay, Thora Hird, Stanley Holloway, Oscar Homolka, Michael Hordern, Walter Huston, Gordon Jackson, Glynis Johns, Celia Johnson, James Mason, James Robertson Justice, Boris Karloff, Jean Kent, Elsa

Lanchester, Charles Laughton, Margaret Lockwood, Herbert Lom, Peter Lorre, Jessie Mathews, Ray Milland, John Mills, Ivor Novello, Lili Palmer, Claude Rains, Basil Rathbone, Michael Redgrave, Michael Rennie, Ralph Richardson, Flora Robson, Patricia Roc, Margaret Rutherford, Harry Secombe, Alistair Sim, Jean Simmons, Conrad Veidt, Jack Warner, Googie Withers, Michael Wilding, and Fay Wray.

In 1935 Gaumont British spent more on film production than any of their competitors. This is a comparison of the cost of British film production in that year. Gaumont British spent £1,200,000, which averaged at £50,000 per film. British International spent £900,000 at Elstree. Associated Talking Pictures (Basil Dean) spent £750,000 at Ealing. London Films (Alexander Korda) spent £500,000. And British & Dominion spent £400,000.

In 1938, ten years after Isidore had launched the corporation, Gaumont British had an issued share and loan capital of £11,187,496 (equivalent to £523,686,687 in 2008).

Chapter 17: SUBSIDIARY COMPANIES

Gaumont British owned control of sixty-eight subsidiary companies including Gainsborough Pictures (1928) Limited, Standard Film Company, Provincial Cinematograph Theatres, Denman Picture Houses, Gaumont British Distributors. In this section I am only mentioning three of the subsidiary companies, otherwise I would never finish writing this book.

British Acoustic Films Limited was the Gaumont British subsidiary that developed, manufactured and installed the talkie equipment they used. Other systems confined the sound to a narrow strip beside the picture on the film. The British Acoustic system used two films of equal width, thus it kept the picture to the standard size and used a separate film of the same width exclusively for the sound. The considerably greater width of the sound strip provided an increased fidelity in the reproduction.

Initially Gaumont British was forced to place a small order with the Western Electric Company for their talkie apparatus. Isidore had completed his arrangements with Siemens and AEG in Germany to use their patents in the manufacture of recording and projection equipment in England. Meanwhile his competitors were using American equipment in their cinemas, so he had to use Western Electric as a stopgap until Gaumont's British Acoustic apparatus was in production.

When the talkies came in the initial cost of installing sound equipment in each cinema was £4,000 (equivalent to £184,560 in 2008) plus an annual service fee of £300 (equivalent to £14,000 in 2008). Gaumont British supplied its own equipment and thereby saved about £400,000 (equivalent to £18,500,000 in 2008), and was not beholden to the powerful American electrical companies.

In 1936 British Acoustic won a lawsuit for infringement of its patents, and was paid damages by the Radio Corporation of America (RCA) who were forced to change their recording equipment in Hollywood.

In 1938 British Acoustic filed another suit in the District Court in Wilmington, Delaware against a subsidiary of RCA and against a subsidiary of Western Electric which was a subsidiary of American Telephone & Telegraph Company (AT&T). British Acoustic sought an injunction to prevent the two defendant companies manufacturing and distributing talkie equipment which may infringe patents they owned. The damages claimed were in excess of £2,000,000 (equivalent to £100,000,000 in 2008), and the outcome would affect every cinema in

America. Improvements in sound equipment manufactured by the defendants were alleged to use British Acoustic patented designs.

Maurice told me they lost this case and did not get the injunction.

Another subsidiary, GB Screen Services Limited, was formed in 1933 to undertake the production and distribution of screen advertising and publicity films. Basil Davies resigned his directorships in Messrs Publicity Films Limited and the London Press Exchange to fully use his specialised expertise in running the new company.

In 1935 GB Instructional Films (GBI) spent £500 making one film a week for showing in schools and institutes in either 35mm or 16mm format. Bruce Woolfe was head of the company, and he initiated the idea of film pictorial text-books for schools.. Another company, GB Equipments (GBE), had a five-year plan to open up schools and institutes and regular cinemas to show documentary films, when necessary supplying sound projectors from 35mm to 16mm "suitcase" talkies. £150,000 had been invested in these two companies, and most of the money came personally from Isidore. At the time GBI and GBE together were the only organisation in the world that could handle the educational and industrial market from production to projection.

Chapter 18: TELEVISION

Isidore wanted to take an interest in the development of radio and television (to get in on the ground floor), and so he formed Bush Radio as a private company, in which Gaumont British owned 40 percent of the shares, and 50 percent was owned by GB directors and their families. Presumably the name Bush is Shepherd's Bush, which is around the corner from Lime Grove.

John Logie Baird, who invented the first working television system, worked from his small laboratory at 22 Frith Street in Soho. Baird's first television transmission was in 1925, and three years later, in 1928, his first colour transmission. In 1927 he

John Logie Baird and Sydney Moseley
in Cannes in 1938
(by kind permission of Malcolm Baird)

formed the Baird Television Development Company
Limited.

Sydney Moseley was at school with Isidore, and he acted as a liaison between Baird and Isidore, who bought control of the Baird Television Company in 1932. He wanted the Baird company to develop and install projection television systems in the larger cinemas so that sporting events could be viewed live as they happened. In 1931 Baird had demonstrated a theatre projection system with a screen of 5 foot wide by 2 foot high. By 1939 he had improved the theatre projection system with a screen of 16 foot wide by 12 foot high. Eventually Isidore wanted to replace the newsreel shown in the cinemas with a televised newsreel, thus doing away with the processing and transporting of reels of film. And his long-term plan was to televise films directly from the studio to the cinema.

By 1934 there were three companies interested in the development of television, and all three had been conducting experiments in secret. Baird, and its rival, Electric and Musical Industries Limited (EMI), had both already produced practical apparatus. A substantial holding in EMI was owned by the Radio Corporation of America (RCA) whose President, David Sarnoff, was a director of EMI as well as being Chairman of the Radio-Keith-Orpheum Corporation (RKO). The new kid on the block was A C Cossor Limited, who pioneered the cathode ray tube.

There was an element of friction between Isidore and Baird because the latter wanted to merge the company with the Marconi Company and later with the General Electric Company. Isidore blocked both of these attempted mergers.

In 1934 Baird displayed his telecine machine for recording television on film using a cathode ray tube and cine camera. The images were developed and dried within two minutes ready to project onto the screen.

Up to 1934 television involved BBC transmissions

using the Baird 30-line system. In 1934 the BBC ended their contract with the Baird Company. Baird obtained permission from the Postmaster General to broadcast experimentally from Crystal Palace, independent from the BBC.

In 1935 the BBC started broadcasting from Alexandra Palace for two hours a day. They alternated transmission times equally between the Baird system and the EMI system. The BBC would assess both systems, and then choose the one they preferred. In 1936 the Crystal Palace was destroyed by fire. Arson was suspected, but the cause of the fire was never discovered. Nevertheless, the fire did occur at an opportune moment for Baird's adversary to advance their rival system. And, in 1937 the BBC stopped broadcasting the Baird system, in favour of the EMI 405-line system.

Renee, my mother, told me that she remembered watching the coronation parade of 1937 on television. Gaumont British covered the parade with their newsreel cameras, but also with their eight television cameras. They did not have permission to broadcast the coronation to the general public, but did so on an experimental basis to the three television sets in the homes of the three Ostrer brothers. She recalled it was a small screen with low definition, but nevertheless an exciting privilege at the time.

The Baird company continued manufacturing television sets for home use, and continued developing, manufacturing and installing projection units for cinemas.

In February 1939 Gaumont British's public service television began at the Tatler cinema in Charing Cross Road and the Marble Arch Pavilion cinema, projected onto a 16 foot wide by 12 foot high screen, and later in the Tivoli cinema onto a 20 foot screen.

The Baird projection system was installed in cinemas in New York including the Roxy and the Embassy.

In 1939 EMI demonstrated their new system using two projectors onto a 16 foot wide by 12 foot high screen. They claimed greater clarity of definition and increased brightness.

Isidore wanted major sporting events (the Derby, the Boat Race, etc.) to be shown in cinemas but required permission from the Postmaster General who insisted that the BBC should have sole responsibility for television broadcasts. Isidore asserted that the BBC was inadequately funded to do the job properly at that time. They covered the boat race with only two cameras, showing just the start and finish, whereas Gaumont British would have used eight along the course to provide a consecutive view of the event.

By 1939 Isidore expressed the opinion that the development of home television would eventually reduce cinema takings. He began installing television projectors in 40 cinemas in and around London, to project television onto the screen with or without permission. Meanwhile the BBC broadcasting monopoly was insistent on keeping television out of cinemas. In 1939 the BBC television only reached 10,000 homes in the London area. Isidore said the BBC was a badly financed, poorly equipped monopoly, whereas Gaumont British could raise the £10,000,000 (equivalent to £495,000,000 in 2008) necessary to erect stations around the country costing the taxpayer nothing. His offer was rejected. In my opinion whether it cost millions or nothing would not have been a consideration because politicians tend to look upon the taxpayer as a cashcow; an unlimited source of finance.

World War Two halted further development of television for the duration, and Isidore sold control of Gaumont British, thus ending his interest in television.

Chapter 19: SUNDAY REFEREE

So far I have covered the Lime Grove studio complex, a few of Gaumont British's subsidiary companies, and it's television interests. Now I am covering Isidore's personal venture into newspaper publishing.

The Sunday Referee newspaper, founded in 1877, was bought by Isidore in 1931. The weekly circulation in May 1937 was certified at 402,652. Mark Goulden, the managing editor, resigned in 1935 over a difference of opinion with Mr Ostrer on a question of major policy. Gosh, there seem to have been several resignations in this story over a difference of opinion with Isidore. Kind of looks like, you either agree with his policy, or you are out the door.

Isidore became the new editor himself. Goulden's position had involved much anxiety because Isidore had insisted on continuing to publish listings for sponsored radio programs in defiance of the Newspaper Proprietors' Association who expelled the Referee from membership, but later reinstated the newspaper. During the period of expulsion new arrangements had to be made regarding distribution because the Association had withdrawn railway train facilities.

The British Broadcasting Corporation (BBC) had a government monopoly on radio broadcasting, and banned the advertising of programs. So advertisers sponsored English-speaking programs from France (or Luxembourg), thereby providing the British public with commercial radio. Most British newspapers were against radio advertising and consistently refused to print the names of the advertisers. Presumably they believed that radio advertising deprived them of advertising revenue. In 1933 The Sunday Referee, in other words Isidore, refused to be coerced and defied the BBC by printing the program details for these commercial broadcasts from France.

In 1935 there were protests from journalists against Lord Beaverbrook (Sunday Express) and Isidore Ostrer (Sunday Referee) because they both invited readers to act as reporters and cameramen, and offered to pay these readers if their services were used. Needless to add, the National Union of Journalists were not happy about articles written by the general public (who were not members of their union) being published.

In 1939 Isidore sold the Sunday Referee to Allied Newspapers, thus ending his involvement in newspaper proprietorship.

Chapter 20: GAUMONT YIDDISH

In May 1931 Isidore's solicitors wrote to the government offering to give his voting shares to the nation. The offer was not accepted. No reason was given, but I assume it was considered inappropriate for the government to control one film company in competition with other such businesses. The government attitude toward broadcasting (radio and television) at the time was monopolistic; to own and control everything. Presumably they did not wish to be in the same situation with film production, distribution and cinemas, which after all provided a considerable amount of tax revenue. For example, in 1931 Gaumont British paid more than £1,000,000 (equivalent to £48,000,000 in 2008) in entertainments tax.

To be a politician does not require qualifications or integrity. An aptitude to con the public effectively whilst skilfully filling your own pockets, seems to me to be the order of the day. They are above the law, and those at the top table never accept responsibility for the numerous errors of judgement they make. Such people are not ideal to decide who should or should not run an industry. Fortunately in the case of Gaumont British, they kept their hands off. Not only was Isidore's offer not accepted, but the offer was withheld from the media for a number of years.

In September 1934 a civil service document said "GB is …. known in the trade as Gaumont-Yiddish". I was absolutely horrified to come across such a blatantly anti-Semitic comment in a government document. And, was somewhat surprised to learn that civil servants spent their time sniffing about "in the trade" to pick up bits of gossip. I can see how this information would have been relevant in Nazi Germany at that time, but not in England. The religious background of businessmen running a company cannot possibly be of interest to anyone other than a bigot.

I am not aware of my father or Isidore or any of my other Uncles ever going to a synagogue. Whether they were Jewish or not is debatable. They did not practice any religion. They all married non-Jewish women, and none of their children were brought up in any religion in particular. Mind you, the public boarding school I attended was sort-of Church of England in my day (God knows what it is now), and it was compulsory to attend a chapel service on Sunday. Not really religion, more like a bit of organ music and a sing along before Sunday luncheon. And during the boring bits (the bible and sermon stuff) one just faded away into one's own private thoughts or emerging teenage sexual fantasies.

My father once told me that religion was a very profitable business with special tax concessions.

And I must confess I briefly entertained the idea of starting my own religion but abandoned it because the prospect of getting any followers, even one, was too daunting. After all the competition relies on indoctrinating or grooming young children whereas I would have to rely on converts, which is much more difficult.

I could never understand why religious people grovel on the floor mumbling pre-learned prayers. After all if individuals could communicate directly with God through prayer, then there is no need for intermediaries, in which case the controlling and money-making religious enterprises are redundant.

Some years ago a friend of mine, Peter, died. Before he left he asked me to arrange his funeral, and specified that he wanted a Jewish service. I had never been to a synagogue in my life and had no idea what was involved, but I made an appointment to see a Rabbi. Of course I selected a Reform Rabbi as I felt sure there would be no point in talking to a representative of the more extreme variation of the faith. The Rabbi asked if Peter was Jewish. No, he wasn't., I replied. I cannot possibly bury a non-Jewish person in consecrated ground, she replied. I am not talking about interment because he is going to be cremated. All I am asking you to do is conduct the service with a Jewish flavour. Absolutely not, she replied, he was not Jewish. I didn't quite see why there was a problem because I understood God created everyone (including non-Jewish people) so surely He would be less discriminatory about such details. Anyway I realised I was wasting my time and went back to the funeral director for advice. He offered me a nun who he said would dress up in anything (presumably within reason) and say whatever I wanted. Fantastic. So I settled for the Jewish Prayer for the Dead, a bit of Khalil Gibran's The Prophet, and Peter's favourite music, Friends of Mr Cairo by Vangelis. And to top it off, I went in search of a Menorah, found a large old silver-plated one which looked great on top of the coffin with tall beeswax candles.   When the proceeding had concluded I jumped up and snatched the Menorah and candles, which now adorns my kitchen mantelpiece.

Chapter 21: ISIDORE CLOSED STUDIO

Isidore said American films shown here take between £7,000,000 and £10,000,000 from Britain every year, but British films shown in America take less than £200,000. He added that unless we can increase our revenue from America, we must discontinue film production.

In 1936 production at Lime Grove was cut. Instead of making 5 or 6 films at the same time, production was cut to no more than 2 films at a time. With only one or two units working at the same time, there was a cut back in staff with considerable economies.

The Film Quota Act of 1927 had proven ineffective in protecting British film production from Hollywood.

So, in 1937 the government was testing the water before introducing its Cinematograph Films Bill. A proposed amendment called the "Separate Quota" was considered. It required distributors to buy 15 per cent of British films annually, and required the cinemas to show 10 per cent of British films. Another proposed amendment called "Reciprocity" was also considered. It required for every seven American films shown in British cinemas, at least two British films must be shown in America. Another proposed amendment suggested to replace the quota proposals with a "Reel Tax" on imported films producing revenue to offset losses on quality British films.

Maurice, my father, who was managing director of Gainsborough Pictures, said at the time the government's quota plan would create a large number of "quota quickies" of insufficient merit to be shown in America. America threatened retaliation by classifying their films "A" or "B". "A" films were top grade to be shown in cinemas on a percentage basis, and "B" films to be hired for a flat sum. The result was to enforce a single-feature program. The Cinematograph Exhibitor's Association declared unless the American scheme was withdrawn, they would not book any "A" films at all, only "B" films. The battle lines had been drawn. The Cinematograph Exhibitor's Association representing the cinemas gave their members a list of new "A" films every week, urging them not to book these films, and a list of new "B" films. The Kinematograph Renters' Society representing the film distributors asked their members not to offer any films at all to certain cinema circuits.

In 1937 Isidore announced that unless a reciprocal agreement is introduced compelling America to buy British films to a value of 25 per cent of the amount taken by them from Britain, Gaumont British will stop film production and close down its studios to consolidate its position.

In 1935 Charles Woolf was paid £20,000 a year (equivalent to £1,050,600 in 2008) He resigned due to "friendly differences", and received £18,000 for termination of his contract. He rented an office in Cork Street, employed a staff of three, and started another production and distribution company called General Films. Within a year he had acquired control of Universal in Hollywood, had opened a big headquarters in Wardour Street in Soho, and was involved in opening Pinewood studios. Woolf had secured backing from paper magnate Lord Portal and flour millionaire J Arthur Rank. In 1937 he signed an agreement with Isidore under which the next eight Gaumont British films would be made at Pinewood.

Isidore closed the Lime Grove studio in March 1937, which involved a reduction of staff, though a number of these employees were absorbed when film production began at Pinewood. Isidore had signed an agreement with Charles Woolf's General Film Distributors from which the corporation received a guaranteed annual income of £130,000 for films produced at Pinewood.

In 1938 the Gainsborough studios in Islington were taken over by Twentieth Century Productions Limited initiating a large expenditure project producing a safe income for Gaumont British without any capital outlay. In other words they rented out the studio facility.

During the two and a half years that Lime Grove was shut they continued to make documentary films, and the laboratories remained open where they printed the newsreels.

Lime Grove reopened in 1939. Woolf died in December 1942

Chapter 22: MAXWELL SUES OSTRERS

Maxwell was a real thorn in the side of the Ostrers; an on-going pain in the neck. He was a real shit, stirring whenever he could. He sued them and lost. He tried to prevent them paying the preference shareholders' dividend, but failed. He stirred up a shareholders revolt to instigate a Board of Trade enquiry into the running of Gaumont British. In fact the only thing that stopped his antagonistic ploys was when he dropped dead. And, in case you are wondering, No, they did not have him rubbed out.

In December 1936 there was a discussion between Joseph M Schenck, who was chairman of 20th Century Fox, His brother, Nicholas Schenck, who was president of Loews (which controlled

Metro-Goldwyn-Mayer), Isidore Ostrer, president of Gaumont British, and my father, Maurice Ostrer. The agenda was the control of Gaumont British, but the talks ended without conclusion because Maurice insisted that John Maxwell should remain in the picture, whereas Joseph Schenck was adamant that Maxwell be eliminated. Thus MGM's negotiation to acquire an interest in the control of Gaumont British fell through.

Later the Ostrer Brothers sold their non-voting 250,000 "B" shares in Metropolis and Bradford to the Associated British Picture Corporation for £1,250,000 (£350,000 cash and 300,000 Associated British ordinary shares). John Maxwell was the chairman and managing director of Associated British, and after this deal he became a director of Gaumont British, though he resigned within a year. He was an ex-lawyer from Glasgow, untidy and casual, arrived at work midday. Associated British Pictures started

John Maxwell in 1936.
(by kind permission of
David Savill/Hulton Archive/Getty Images)

in 1926 as M E Productions, and in 1927 became British International Pictures, and in 1933 it bought Associated British Cinemas. Associated British Pictures became Maxwell's holding company to control British International Pictures, Associated British Cinemas, Wardour Films, Pathe Pictures, and British Instructional Films. Maxwell's company owned the studios at Elstree and Welwyn, and a portfolio of 283 cinemas. It was said, if you criticised Maxwell, his shareholders would tear you apart, whereas the Gaumont British shareholders seemed more inclined to tear the Ostrers apart.

Gaumont British had its own releasing organisation in America, but the actual physical distribution was through 20th Century Fox by special arrangement. However, Sidney R Kent, president of 20th Century Fox, declared that his company will refuse to distribute films that were not actual Gaumont British productions. Kent's announcement was a direct challenge to John Maxwell, who had recently been elected to the board of Gaumont British and had subsequently suggested the GB organisation in America ought distribute all good British films including those made at Maxwell's Associated British studio. Kent effectively blocked that proposition. Schenck had objected to Maxwell buying in.

After Maxwell had bought into the Metropolitan & Bradford Trust, the holding company that controlled Gaumont British, he had become a director of Gaumont British. Four GB directors, who were outvoted, tried to prevent the company paying the half-year dividend to the preference shareholders. These four, including Maxwell, were fighting for control of the company. If the dividend fell six months in arrears, then the preference shareholders were entitled to vote which could have removed control from the Ostrers. The point of argument was that some of the subsidiary companies made losses, whereas others made profits which were more than adequate to meet the preference dividend. I suspect the argument was somewhat contrived to rock the boat, hoping the captain would fall overboard. The dissenting directors sought counsel's advice on the matter.

In 1937 a court refused an injunction to restrain payment of the Gaumont British preference dividend. The action brought by a shareholder was dismissed with costs.

In 1938 John Maxwell's Associated British Picture Corporation sued the Ostrer brothers (Isidore, Mark & Maurice) claiming £600,000 damages (equivalent to £30,000,000 in 2008) for alleged fraudulent misrepresentation. He alleged that representations had been made to him concerning Gaumont British profits that were not correct. He claimed he had been induced to buy shares in the Metropolitan & Bradford Trust.

Lawrence Howard also sued the Ostrer brothers

claiming £50,000 damages, which he alleged was the agreed remuneration for negotiating the sale of the Ostrer's shares in the Metropolitan & Bradford Trust to Maxwell. This case was settled out of court for an agreed sum with costs.

Maxwell claimed that representations had been made to him by the three Ostrers that the Gaumont British profits for the year ended March 1936 were £700,000, the same amount as in the previous year. The balance sheet had not yet been published, but when it was it showed the same amount of profit. Later when he sat as a Gaumont British director he saw the detailed schedules from which the balance sheet had been prepared and took the view that the published balance sheet was inaccurate. However, the report of the independent auditors endorsed the accuracy of the published balance sheet.

Counsel for the defendants pointed out that Maxwell

had bought a large holding in the Metropolitan & Bradford Trust, but not control. He had a five-year option to buy the controlling shares for £900,000 (equivalent to £47,000,000 in 2008), but the American shareholders (Fox) prevented him from exercising this option. He then suggested he had been misled in the purchase of these shares because he claimed the deal was conditional on a promise from Isidore that he would persuade Fox to sell their holding. Maxwell later claimed fraud. Judgement was entered for the Ostrer brothers with costs. Shortly afterward John Maxwell resigned his directorship in Gaumont British.

At the annual meeting in 1937, Isidore announced a net loss for the year of £566,800 on production and distribution of films. The profit from the cinemas was greater than the loss from production and distribution, and so he decided to close down the studio complex at Lime Grove to consolidate and stabilise Gaumont British's financial future.

Isidore also announced he had signed an agreement with General Film Distributors from which the corporation would receive a guaranteed annual income of £130,000 for films produced at Pinewood without any capital outlay. I mentioned this agreement in more detail earlier in this book.

C L Nordon, a solicitor, said he represented shares worth £500,000 and he criticised various items in the balance sheet. There were shouts of "Sit down". Nordon responded: "Large numbers of those here are employees of the company. I do not think it right for them to interrupt." One shareholder shouted: "I have every penny in the company, and I am an employee". Nordon moved his amendment to reject the accounts. W H J Drown rose to second. The amendment was defeated. Isidore closed the meeting saying: "You have been very splendid in the way you have helped us through a very difficult meeting."

After the annual meeting, Nordon, acting on behalf of certain shareholders who had formed themselves into a provisional committee, wrote to Gaumont British's Secretary requesting the co-opting of new directors to represent the independent shareholders and an investigation of the companies accounts, and 18 further queries. The letter ended saying unless Nordon received a satisfactory reply within seven days, he will requisition an extra-ordinary general meeting, and will apply for a Board of Trade inspector to investigate the matter.

The company's Secretary replied to Nordon requesting the number and shareholding of his provisional committee. Furthermore he said the information requested in Nordon's letter went far beyond anything reasonably required in an investigation of the company's accounts, therefore for what purpose was this information required.

Nordon replied he was expressly instructed not to

divulge the names of the shareholders in case public criticism is directed against them. If a satisfactory assurance is given that no personal reference is made to these shareholders, he will obtain authority to disclose their names and shareholdings, but some of them hold shares in nominees' names.

Gaumont British's solicitor replied to Nordon saying he had neglected to state the purpose of each of the 18 points in his original letter. Furthermore, it is impossible to give an assurance that no criticism will be made against these shareholders without knowing who they are. At the annual meeting, less than one per cent of the shareholding voted against acceptance of the accounts, therefore it is an exaggeration for Nordon to claim his committee represents a large dissenting body.

A further attempt to instigate a Board of Trade enquiry was made by W H J Drown, chairman of the shareholders' committee. He petitioned the company's shareholders with several circulars, and obtained the necessary 10 per cent required to support his application.

In the House of Commons, Sir Arnold Wilson MP asked the President of the Board of Trade if he was aware that Gaumont British was in the hands of three persons (the Ostrer brothers) one of whom was an unnaturalised alien, and asked him to consider restoring control to British shareholders. In a counter-statement Isidore referred to a concerted attack on the policy and management of the corporation and ill-founded gossip about his own nationality.

In 1939, as a result of the two-year agitation by Drown and Nordon, the Board of Trade appointed an official inspector to investigate Gaumont British's affairs. No doubt Isidore would have liked to drown Mr Drown. Tom Williams MP asked the President of the Board of Trade if he had acceded to the repeated requests from 90 per cent of the shareholders for facilities to prove malicious intent of the persons who had applied for the investigation.

In 1940 Mark Ostrer refused to give evidence in the presence of a shorthand stenographer because the information was commercially confidential. Charles Harman KC, acting for Mark Ostrer, said the applicants of this case were a small minority of shareholders who were moved, influenced or headed by John Maxwell, who was managing director of the chief competitor company. And one of the objects of the application was to obtain information about the affairs of Gaumont British that would be useful to this competitor.

Maxwell died in 1940. And, the Ostrers sold control of Gaumont British.

Chapter 23: ISIDORE SELLS CONTROL

To recapitulate. Lets face it, for years Uncle Isidore had been waving this golden carrot around, and most of his biggest competitors squabbled amongst themselves to grab it. The golden carrot was the 5,100 £1 "A" voting shares in his private holding company, the Metropolis and Bradford Trust. This block of shares controlled the Gaumont British Picture Corporation, the studios, the distribution companies, the cinema circuits, the subsidiary companies, the lot. First Fox wanted the block of shares, but didn't get it. They paid £4,000,000 and ended up with a lot of non-voting shares, and a lesser number of voting shares. Next John Maxwell of Associated British Pictures paid £350,000 (plus a pile of ABP stock) for the remaining non-voting shares and an option to buy the "A" voting shares. But Fox said Maxwell cannot buy the voting shares without their permission. So both Fox and Maxwell wanted the block of voting shares, but neither of them got it. Instead they paid for a load of non-voting shares and a seat on the board of GB. But within a year Maxwell resigned from the board. Next Philip Hill, the financier behind Oscar Deutsch of Odeon Theatres Limited backed Deutsch in an unsuccessful offer for Gaumont British. The Fox interest was opposed to Deutsch's offer.

Oscar Deutsch was short, plump, bald, and vivacious. He was a workaholic, and was often seen in white-tie-and-tails in the foyer of the Dorchester Hotel in Park Lane until 2 am talking business. Deutsch always went home to Birmingham week-ends, where he was a metal merchant. His wife designed the interior of each new Odeon cinema in a distinct and recognisable art-deco style, that stood

**J Arthur Rank (centre front) with his family
at his house, Aldwick Place, West Sussex.
(by kind permission John Rank)**

out from the palatial grandeur of other cinemas of the time.

In 1938 J. Arthur Rank was chairman of the General Cinema Finance Corporation, and bought Denham Studios, and in 1939 bought Elstree. Deutsch died in 1941, and Rank bought Odeon from his widow. The Ostrers sold Gaumont British to Rank for £750,000 in

1940, finalised in 1941. (equivalent to £39,400,000 in 2008), but the transfer of control was completed in 1944. Isidore spent the war years in Arizona.

Isidore was the brains behind Gaumont British, working discreetly in the background, while Mark was the front man, Maurice was Isidore's shadow, David was sales, Harry was scripts. Film star James Mason (married to my cousin) once said the five Ostrer brothers had one opinion and one brain. That sounds about right. Or, to put it another way, Isidore was the puppeteer pulling the strings, and the rest were an assortment of marionettes.

Isidore built a pyramid in which £5,000 (£245,000 in 2008) voting shares in a holding company controlled Gaumont British worth £13,000,000 (£640,000,000 in 2008). I feel he was a builder who created an empire and dealt with the problems as they arose. He enjoyed planning, scheming and manipulating to create his empire, and so he was in his element orchestrating take-overs and absorbing them in the expanding kingdom he was building. But, he was bored by the day-to-day running of the business. He would delegate these mundane functions to lesser mortals, whilst retaining overall control. Thus he would never fully delegate. As a result most of the talented experts running the various departments in the business, eventually resigned. They found it too frustrating to fulfil their duties with the back-room interference. To make matters worse, Isidore (like God) was unapproachable. You had to communicate with him through his brothers (equivalent to the clergy).

My research for this book has revealed that Isidore was an entirely different person before the Second World War, in the late 1920s and the 1930s. From his beginnings in poverty, he had built up a vast personal fortune. He was an ambitious entrepreneur, and quite extravert. He presided over annual meetings calming the shareholders into accepting no dividend. He invited the press to his home, reading a statement to sixteen journalists. He weathered the storm after making 700 employees redundant in the mid 1930s at the height of the depression. He survived law suits and survived threatened government enquiries. I reckon the energy and the stress of this undertaking, burnt him out, and he withdrew into himself and became a recluse, pottering about, eating bananas, drinking carrot juice and writing poetry, and doing the odd painting as one does in retirement.

My father, Maurice Ostrer, was a director of both the corporation and Gainsborough, and acted in the capacity of liaison officer. He held thirty-three directorships in the Gaumont British group of companies and subsidiaries. Later, he was executive film producer. My mother acted in eleven films under her maiden name, Renee Clama, until she married in 1933.

During World War Two air raids and transport difficulties disrupted film production. Maurice was in charge of production at the time, and he offered studio staff the chance to live in at the studio. He arranged for wives and children to be evacuated to a safe area, providing communal accommodation, and he proposed a five-day working week, so that everyone could spend the full weekend with their family, enjoying recreation and rest. The workers met with Maurice to discuss the proposals. Maurice had a bed installed in his office for the duration.

Maurice stayed on with Rank until 1946. During the 1940s Gaumont British produced some of its most highly acclaimed films, and it is said under Rank directors enjoyed complete artistic freedom plus suitably endowed budgets to create the best films. Rank renamed most of the Gaumont cinemas as Odeon, but a number survived with the name Gaumont into the 1960s and 1970s, and a few into the 1980s. There are no cinemas named Gaumont left in Britain today, not one. They have all long gone to become Odeons, or bingo halls, or multiplexes, or have been demolished. Many of the films have also gone, either lost or disintegrated. After the last Gainsborough film was made in 1950, Rank sold the Lime Grove studio complex to the British Broadcasting Corporation who used it for 40 years as a television studio. Later, in the 1990s, when they had built their own vast facility in nearby Wood Lane, the 1932 complex was sold to a property developer, who demolished the listed building and constructed a clump of small terraced houses on the site. All that remains of Gaumont British, now faded into the dust of history, is two road signs attached to one of the small houses.

**Clump of small houses with Road Signs that replaced
the demolished Gaumont British studio complex.
(by kind permission of the Ostrer Family Archive)**

The monumental human endeavour driven by the hard work, inspiration and enthusiasm of so many talented people made this corporation become Britain's biggest film production company in the 1930s. To-day, the names Gaumont and Gaumont British have in effect been airbrushed out of British film history, only remembered by the few survivors whose lives it touched.

Chapter 24: ILLINGWORTH MORRIS

In 1920 the Ostrer Brothers merchant bank floated Amalgamated Textiles Limited (Amalgamated) which acquired control of three textile companies: William Morris & Sons Limited, John H Beaver Limited and Daniel Illingworth & Sons Limited. A year later Isidore changed the name of Amalgamated to Illingworth, Morris & Company Limited (IM). And in 1923 he increased the share capital of IM to £5,000,000 (equivalent to £209,000,000 in 2008).

During the 1920s and 1930s Isidore was focused on creating, expanding, and running Gaumont British. And so IM was on the back burner until after World War Two. In 1954 IM bought John Smith (Field Head) Limited, and Salts (Saltaire) Limited in 1958.

Salts'subsidiaries included J & J Crombie Limited, Josiah France Limited, Pepper Lee & Company Limited and James Sykes & Sons Limited. My father, Maurice told me that the Salts Group of companies was larger than the rest of IM. Later IM bought Joshua Hoyle & Sons Limited, which I visited with my father. And while I was studying at Leeds University I visited Salts.

The controlling shares in IM was held by each of the three Ostrer brothers (Isidore, Mark and Maurice) and by two private holding companies: Lothbury Investment Corporation Limited (Lothbury) and LOG Trust Limited (LOG). G R Mackay (a partner in the chartered accountant's firm: Rawlinson & Hunter) was elected onto the Board of IM in 1946 as a nominee representing the Ostrers. In 1951 Mark Ostrer became a director of IM, and Lord Wilmot became Chairman of the Board. My father, Maurice, succeeded Uncle Mark on the Board. And when Wilmot died in 1964, my father became Chairman.

Needless to add, throughout Isidore was controlling the proceedings from off-stage.

In 1970 the then managing director of IM told me that though Isidore had owned control of Illingworth Morris for 50 years, he had never visited Yorkshire or any of the mills. To Isidore running his textile empire was a matter of juggling bits and pieces around on a balance sheet. He didn't need physical contact with the production facility.   And when necessary, executives would visit him at Hills End for instructions. In other words, he ran it from his home.

Isidore's textile empire, Illingworth Morris, eventually owned 52 mills, and was one of the largest such groups in the world. Just like Gaumont British, IM was controlled from a private holding company, Lothbury Trust,. Again there were a large number of non-voting shares to provide capital for expansion, and a smaller number of voting shares to control the enterprise, and a huge loan, which Isidore told me was in the region of £12,000,000 (equivalent to £145,000,000 in 2008).

Lightning Source UK Ltd.
Milton Keynes UK
06 January 2011

165263UK00001B/227/P

9 780956 482211